Coaching Soccer Like Guardiola and Mourinho

For all those to whom soccer is more than just a game!

Be positive – Timo Jankowski, April 2015

Timo Jankowski

COACHING
SOCCER
LIKE GUARDIOLA AND MOURINHO

The Concept of Tactical Periodization

Meyer & Meyer Sport

Original title: Taktische Periodisierung im Fußball, Aachen: Meyer & Meyer Verlag
Translation: AAA Translations, St. Louis, Missouri

British Library Cataloguing in Publication Data

A catalogue record for this book is available from the British Library

Coaching Soccer like Guardiola and Mourinho

© 2016 by Meyer & Meyer Verlag, Aachen

Aachen, Auckland, Beirut, Cairo, Cape Town, Dubai, Hägendorf, Hong Kong,

Indianapolis, Manila, New Delhi, Singapore, Sydney, Tehran, Vienna

Member of the World Sport Publishers' Association (WSPA)

Manufacturing: Print Consult GmbH, Munich, Germany

ISBN 978-1-78255-072-3

E-Mail: info@m-m-sports.com

www.m-m-sports.com

Contents

CHAPTER 1

Work hard and work smart—Facts, trends, "fans," and tactical periodization

CHAPTER 1

Work hard and work smart—
Facts, trends, "fans," and
tactical periodization

"Look at the best, learn from the best, be the best."

World-class peers: Cristiano Ronaldo and Lionel Messi

*M*any coaches, unfortunately, still compare soccer to war in their pre-game motivational speeches.

Since war is something negative, this assertion can only make one chuckle.

Soccer is by definition a *game*.

Tackles, positive aggressiveness, and perseverance certainly play an important role.

But anyone who thinks of soccer as war instead of a game will also structure his training incorrectly, and players will walk away from the sport.

Often coaches with this attitude about soccer have their players run pointless laps around the field while circling their arms or other such military-like drills.

Honestly, how many soccer players have you seen running in circles at the same pace while circling their arms during a game?

Legendary coach Wiel Coerver once said that there is more than one truth in soccer, and many roads lead to a destination:

- Brazil won the World Cup with Joga Bonito.
- Spain won the World Cup with Tiki-Taka.
- Germany won the World Cup with discipline and organization.
- Italy won the World Cup with Catenaccio.
- Argentina won the World Cup with Diego Maradona, and France with Zinedine Zidane.
- The Netherlands has never won the World Cup in spite of Johann Cruyff, Marco van Basten, and Arjen Robben.

Success in soccer is possible with many different methods and game concepts, and that is exactly what makes soccer so interesting and diverse—more so than any other sport.

But, as with economic benchmarking, it is a fact that the best soccer teams and the top players in their respective positions must be painstakingly analyzed with respect to how they play, how they behave, and how they train.

"Anyone who doesn't keep up with the times, in time will be gone."

Soccer and modern training are advancing at a rapid pace.

Even as number games and statistics in soccer are sneered at, one cannot deny the importance—particularly in training—of a soccer coach knowing that, for instance, 80% of all passes are played directly or after only one additional touch, or that 75% of all ball handling in top competitive soccer is done under pressure from behind.

Not to mention that nowadays, depending on the league, approximately 30% of all goals are scored from set pieces.

Tactical genius, Marcelo Bielsa, who coached Chile at the 2010 World Cup, brought along 700 videos with footage of the opposition to South Africa and offered this justification:

"I know that success and luck are not synonymous."

With television and Internet soccer know-how now reaching the most remote corners of the world, the decades-long advantage of the Western soccer world has begun to shrink.

Small nations have made up enormous ground in all areas of soccer, and the level of play continues to even out.

Anyone who doesn't continue to progress is swallowed up by these small nations that are hungry for success.

During the 2014 World Cup, Costa Rica made its way into the quarterfinals, deservedly so, and there had the misfortune of losing against the Netherlands—a great soccer nation—in a penalty shootout.

At the 2014 FIFA Club World Cup, Auckland City FC from the small rugby and cricket nation New Zealand reached the semifinals for the first time, and, with a 4-2 victory in a penalty shootout against the Mexican representatives CD Cruz Azul, ended up taking third place.

Teams from Germany's regional leagues are eliminating Bundesliga teams from the German national championships.

It is also becoming a more frequent occurrence that national teams from countries with small populations, such as the Faroe Islands with less than 50,000 people, deservedly win as visitors with a 1-0 over European champions, such as Greece with a population of 10 million, because these teams also possess very good structures and sponsorship programs.

To make Iceland internationally competitive, many soccer stadiums were built, so, therefore, the game could be played during the cold and dark winter months.

The success of this well-planned system speaks for itself: In 2013, Iceland only foundered against Croatia in the last playoff game of the World Cup after finishing the first leg game with a 0-0 score.

In 2014, the Netherlands, with star players like Arjen Robben, were soundly beaten 2-0 by Iceland in a European Cup qualifying game.

It would be interesting to see what would happen if African countries possessed a better soccer infrastructure or even just a soccer ball for every child.

With the appropriate structures, Olympic soccer champions, Nigeria, with a population of more than 150 million soccer enthusiasts, would likely roll over many European teams.

A single soccer school in Abidjan in the Ivory Coast with a more or less western infrastructure has produced top international players such as Yaya Touré (Manchester City), Kolo Touré (FC Liverpool), Salomon Kalou (Hertha BSC), Emmanuel Eboue (Galatasaray Istanbul), and Arthur Boka (FC Málaga).

But even Ivory Coast with its star players must stay vigilant. At the 2012 Africa Cup of Nations in Gabon and Equatorial Guinea, Ivory Coast lost the final against the perceived outsider Zambia, which, thanks to its charismatic and skilled top soccer coach Hervé Renard, won the tournament with a sound tactical strategy.

At the press conference before the final, Renard spoke of the magic of soccer:

"For eight years I took out the garbage. Today I am here as coach at the Africa Cup final. Isn't soccer magical?"

In 2015, Renard managed the feat of becoming the first coach to win the Africa Cup twice and, as coach for the Ivory Coast national team, beat Ghana in a memorable penalty shootout.

The fact that many so-called fans of the German team at the 2014 World Cup complained about their team's draw against Ghana or the win against Algeria in overtime and how it was possible that the German team was unable to score a decisive victory against these teams can only be attributed to Western arrogance or a complete lack of soccer expertise.

As if soccer were not played in Africa...

In soccer, overall, and in our latitudes, in particular, especially in the German-speaking realm, there exist extremely negative behavior patterns and counterproductive attitudes that are propagated primarily by these so-called fans.

In mid-July, the German national team was frenetically celebrated after its World Cup victory, only to be booed by their own fans scarcely two months later, barely 20 minutes into the game, at a rematch against Argentina that ended in a 2-4 loss.

The author, Tim Jankowski, in Ivory Coast—Despite a zest for life and exceptional talent, often, as in this picture, a single ball is shared by 30 to 40 children.

Much as it has all areas of life, globalization impacts soccer.

African teams defend with as much discipline as Europeans; Europeans make magic like Brazilians; and Brazilians press as a compact unit and counter.

There are extremely skilled head-ball players from Mexico and Chile, whereas some English players struggle with going up in the air.

The 1-4-3-3 formation is no longer just used by the Dutch, and the Netherlands themselves played with a 1-3-5-2 basic formation at the 2014 World Cup.

When analyzing the current best national teams and club teams, one inadvertently finds that nearly all currently successful coaches and teams use a specific form of training planning and control, and they use the same concept for their successes.

In 2014, the European Cup finalists Atlético and Real Madrid, as well as Beneficia Lisbon and FC Sevilla, and the four semifinalists, Bayern Munich, Chelsea London, FC Valencia, and Juventus Torino, all used a very specific training concept:

1.1   THE CONCEPT OF TACTICAL PERIODIZATION

Pep Guardiola and José Mourinho—The two best-known proponents of tactical periodization in planning..

In the top leagues such as the Bundesliga, the English Premiere League, and the Spanish Primera División, the teams that won the title along with FC Bayern Munich, Manchester City, and Atlético Madrid were those whose coaches all rely on the tactical periodization concept.

Next to the two currently most successful coaches in the world, **Pep Guardiola** and **José Mourinho**, many other internationally renowned top coaches also rely on the tactical periodization concept:

- **Louis van Gaal,** one of the most successful coaches in the history of soccer, plans his entirely game-specific trairing based on precisely structured playing concept and tactical principles.

- **Marcelo Bielsa**, currently with Olympique Marseille, who is considered the official role model by no less than Pep Guardiola, employs the principles of Periodização tática..

- **Carlos Queiroz**, who became world champion with Portugal's U-17 and U-20, was assistant coach for Manchester United and head coach for Real Madrid and is currently the national coach for Iraq.

- **André Villas-Boas**, who won the national championship, league cup, and European League with FC Porto and was the head coach for Chelsea London and Tottenham Spurs and is currently with Zenit in St. Petersburg, Russia, swears by tactical periodization.

- **Brendan Rodgers** of Northern Ireland, who is currently the head coach for FC Liverpool and who enthuses with attractive attacking soccer, also does his planning based on key tactical concepts.

- Algeria's national coach, **Christian Gourcouff**, is one of the most eminent tactical experts in France and has been extremely successful with FC Lorient. In his book, *Un autre regard sur le football*, it is apparent that he, too, also relies heavily on tactics.

- **Rudi Garcia**, who currently excites fans with his fabulous attacking soccer at AS Rome and previously at OSC Lille, has a tactical concept on which his training is based. He was awarded France's Coach of the Year in 2011, 2013, and 2014.

- There is a reason why **Mauricio Pochettino** got a five-year contract with the Tottenham Hotspurs. The 20-time Argentinian national player received much attention as coach for Espanyol Barcelona and FC Southampton due to his excellent, tactically structured concept.

- **Roberto Martínez Montoliú**, currently with FC Everton, won the FA Cup in 2013 with Wigan Athletic as an underdog, using the tactical periodization concept.

- **Jorge Luis Pinto**, who provides an insight into his tactical secrets and methods on his website *http://www.jorgeluispinto.com*, reached the World Cup quarterfinals in Brazil and is considered Costa Rica's answer to José Mourinho.

- **Paulo Sousa**, Junior World champion as a player, two-time Champions League winner, and the current successful coach for FC Basel, dominates the Swiss League and also inspires in the Champions League with the tactical periodization concept.

Many more well-known top coaches like Jorge Sampaoli (coach for the Chile national team), Julen Lopetegui (FC Porto), Jorge Jesus (Beneficia Lisbon), or Luis Enrique Martínez García (FC Barcelona) always base their planning on key tactical concepts with much success.

Still, many other soccer coaches plan their training based on outdated models and periodization concepts taken from track and field or other dissimilar disciplines outside the sport of soccer.

When there is no planning at all, training weeks are subdivided into speed and endurance weeks instead of training that is based on soccer-specific key aspects. In the tactical periodization model, even fitness-related factors are always embedded in a tactical concept specific to soccer.

The first part of this book provides a detailed explanation of the different types of periodization models, what exactly is behind this extremely promising concept, and how to specifically apply the principles of tactical periodization.

The second part of the book presents more than 60 selected and carefully researched practice drills used by renowned professional organizations, international youth programs, and top coaches, such as José Mourinho, Pep Guardiola, Louis van Gaal, and Jürgen Klopp.

Specifically, these drills all have an integrated structure similar to soccer, meaning predominant performance factors of tactics, technique, fitness, and mental ability are always absolutely game-specific in order to optimally represent the complexity of the game. In this way, the presented drills are extremely effective.

Enjoy reading, following, challenging, and implementing!

"The only true wisdom is in knowing you know nothing." – Sokrates

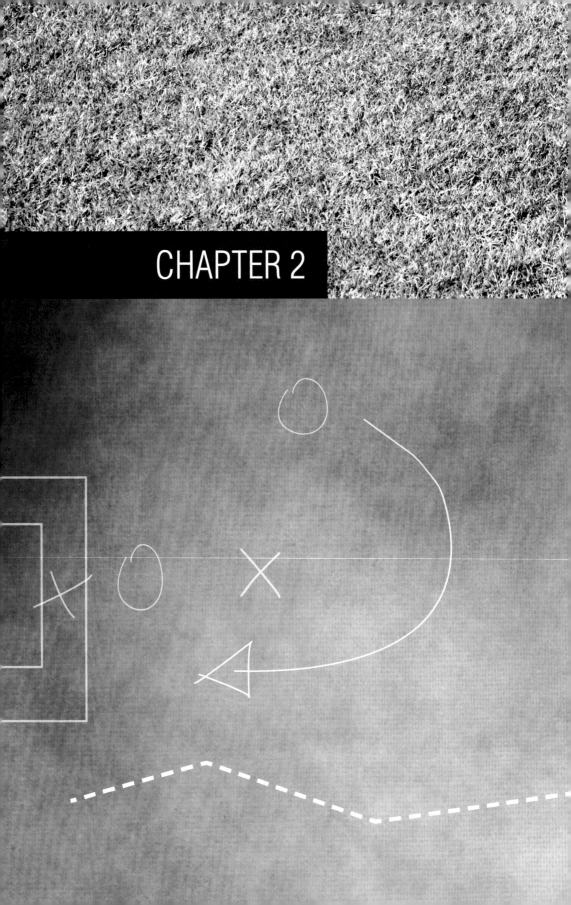

CHAPTER 2

The player who makes the difference—
Self-confidence, self-motivation, humility, pressure to perform, personal development, and positive pushing

The player who makes the difference—Self-confidence, self-motivation, humility, pressure to perform, personal development, and positive pushing

"You need an inner, deep-rooted belief you are good enough. No confidence, no performance."

Confidence or arrogance? The fact is, without confidence, there is no world-class performance. CR7 celebrates his goal in the 2014 Champions League final.

here is no success without planning, but due to soccer's high degree of complexity, losses sometimes happen—even with perfect planning.Die enorme Komplexität wird sehr gut im folgenden Schaubild von Prof. Jürgen Weineck aufgezeigt, in dem die Vielfältigkeit der benötigten Fähigkeiten dargestellt wird.

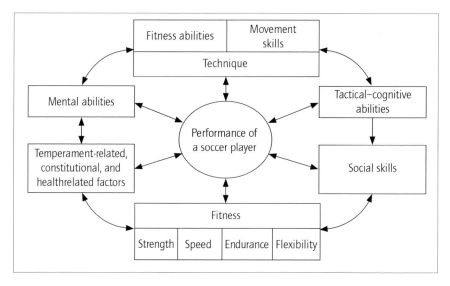

Performance components in soccer as per Dr. Jürgen Weineck (Weineck, J. 2004. Optimal Soccer Training, 4th edition, Balingen: Spitta).

But despite the complexity, the odds of winning can be increased enormously through perfect planning and training, thereby counteracting any coincidence.

As previously mentioned in chapter 1, any planning must begin with a world-ranking analysis:

• **What are the world's best coaches doing, and why are they so successful?**

Objectives for training a soccer player are derived from here.

What must a soccer player's training entail so he can be competitive at the highest level?

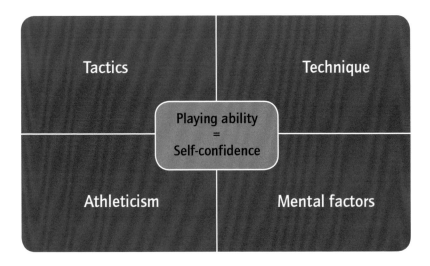

In soccer, there are four major interacting performance factors that must be viewed in an overall context:

- Tactics
- Technique
- Athleticism
- Mental factors

These four major performance factors can then be divided into many sub-factors, which would, however, go beyond the scope of any diagram.

When a player is perfectly trained tactically, technically, athletically, and mentally, he possesses a high level of playing ability.

If the player can effectively bring these abilities to the field, he automatically has self-confidence and, thus, has developed into a player who makes the difference.

Therefore, the ultimate goal in working with soccer players is to teach the players confidence that should, however, never turn into arrogance, which in many cases is a fine line. This is why teaching values such as humility and modesty is of critical importance when working with a soccer team.

Humility = Humility (adjectival form: humble) is seen as the act or attitude of lowering oneself in relation to others or, conversely, having a clear perspective and respect for one's place in context.

Or, as Dettmar Cramer has already noted,

Dettmar Cramer, too, was aware of the importance of tactics and the right attitude

"As long as better is possible, good isn't good enough."

Or, as the record producer and entrepreneur Dieter Bohlen says,
"Anyone who can't do what he wants must want what he can do!"

Virtues such as discipline and humility also played an important role for Joachim Löw in the 2014 World Cup victory, as well as for Pep Guardiola, who largely attributes his great success with FC Barcelona and the superstars surrounding Messi to the internalization of these important virtues.

Ideally, one's own team has more players with self-confidence, the right virtues, and the willingness to take responsibility on the field than the opponent's team.

"Give me the ball. I will decide."

The coach for Arsenal FC, Arsène Wenger, also confirms this approach regarding the training of a soccer player with the following statement:

"At a young age, winning is not the most important thing. The important thing is to develop creative and skilled players with confidence."

Coach Arsène Wenger also puts a lot of emphasis on tactical elements in his training units and is well aware of the importance of self-confidence in soccer.

One of the world's best trainers in youth soccer is the Netherlands' Piet Hamberg, who played for Ajax Amsterdam and Servette Geneva and was the head coach for the youth squads at Grasshoppers Zurich, FC Liverpool, and Red Bull Salzburg. Piet Hamberg endorses this mindset with his approach "House of Talents" in which the management—meaning coaches, support staff, and environment—and the right mentality form the foundation on which all other abilities are built on. Once the realization sets in that a healthy amount of self-confidence is most important when working with soccer players and the other performance factors serve this goal, it will have a huge impact on a coach's planning and coaching.

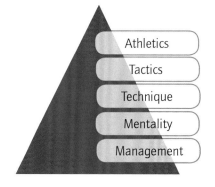

Athletics

Tactics

Technique

Mentality

Management

Training goals now become much clearer, and interactions with the players as well as coaching become much more positive, which contributes to a perfect learning situation in which players can continue to grow.

Now the coach tries to use **positive pushing** with his players, which will have a huge impact on learning progression.

What player or person doesn't like praise and positive encouragement?

Of course, a coach wants to improve his players, and interacting with positive criticism is very important, but it should always be constructive and help the player improve. Applying this knowledge will primarily nurture the players according to their strengths and not merely weed out the weaknesses. Thus, the motto is self-confidence instead of fear, which the coach for FC Everton, Roberto Martínez Montolin, confirms:

"Jugar sien miedo—play without fear!"

Roberto Martínez Montolin

Many coaches use fear as a managerial style, which is never good advice since fear inhibits. Potential can never be fully realized under the influence of fear. Players must know where they stand with their coach. The Spanish World and European Championships coach, Vicente del Bosque, confirms this with the simple statement:

"Siempre igua—always the same" – *Vicente del Bosque*

But fear should not be confused with positive pressure to perform, which is a huge performance-determining factor that must be accepted as a constant concomitant in both soccer and life.

Or, in the words of José Mourinho,

"What pressure? Pressure is when poor people in the third world try to feed their family. There is no pressure in soccer."

José Mourinho— positive interaction with performance pressure

"Champions do EXTRA," or "from nothing comes nothing."

Another noticeable peculiarity in the world ranking analysis that is visually apparent to even soccer amateurs is that nearly all **players who make a difference**, such as Bale, Ronaldo, Ramos, Robben, and Messi, possess a better musculature than 99% of all pro soccer players.

But the visuals are only a positive side effect. These players know that strength is the basis for athletic performance, and a good musculature protects from injury.

That superior muscles are hard earned is underscored by the fact that, as a youth player at the Beneficia Lisbon boarding school, Cristiano Ronaldo would climb through the window of the weight room in order to steel his muscles.

Players who make a difference and model athletes: Gareth Bale and Cristiano Ronaldo—Perfect athletic prerequisites for a soccer player created through countless extra hours and a high degree of self-motivation

In addition, it is important that a coach realizes that while he can "mentally push" players for a short time, this can never be a motivator long-term.

Motivation can only come from the player, which is why **self-motivation**, good **learning ability**, as well as a good **winning mentality** are extremely important talent criteria in soccer.

A player who joins a youth academy at age 8 has 10 years to be shaped technically, tactically, and athletically by top coaches, but in most cases, character is already largely defined in those early years and very difficult to change.

The coach must, therefore, identify players with good learning ability, self-motivation, and the necessary passion and then provide these players with an environment in which they can permanently improve. This is why **personal development** plays such an important role in the training of a soccer player.

How big of a personality does it take for 80,000 spectators and millions of television viewers worldwide to watch a soccer game that is shaped by these personalities?

"Preparation meets opportunity."

While there is more time for personal development in other professions—for instance, a physician who only begins to assume full responsibility at age 30—soccer players often are already on the big stage at age 17 or 18, which is why the process of personal development must take place more quickly.

Responsibility at age 17: Goal-scorer Breel Embolo of FC Basel in the Champions League game against FC Liverpool

"If you are looking for a helping hand, let your eyes wander down your arm…and there it is: the helping hand."

Or, as my father used to say,

"Help yourself, and God will help you!"

Additionally, an important trend in modern soccer is that all successful teams try to play **actively instead of passively**, always and everywhere.

For this reason, soccer players must be taught from a young age through appropriate coaching and the right training content to **shape their destiny themselves rather than passively waiting for it to happen.**

To that end, the correct choice of words is the first step in the right direction.

Instead of the passive word, "defend," it is better to use the active word, "attack."

Instead of "goaltender," who, as the word suggests, merely tends the goal, talk about a "goal player," like Manuel Neuer.

Instead of frightening and inhibiting youth players with statements such as, "Score that damned goal already" (no matter that no one intentionally misses), it is better to say, "No sweat, good try! The next one will go in," and then offer to help the player after the next practice and work on the situation with individual training.

Thus, the most important goals in training a player who makes a difference are

- identifying players with lots of self-motivation, learning ability, and winner mentality;
- building self-confidence while simultaneously imparting important values such as humility, discipline, and modesty;
- exposing players to positive performance pressure and positive pushing;
- shaping soccer players into personalities; and
- being active instead of passive to shape one's own destiny.

Personal development in soccer—David Beckham also assumes responsibility off the soccer field as a UNICEF ambassador.

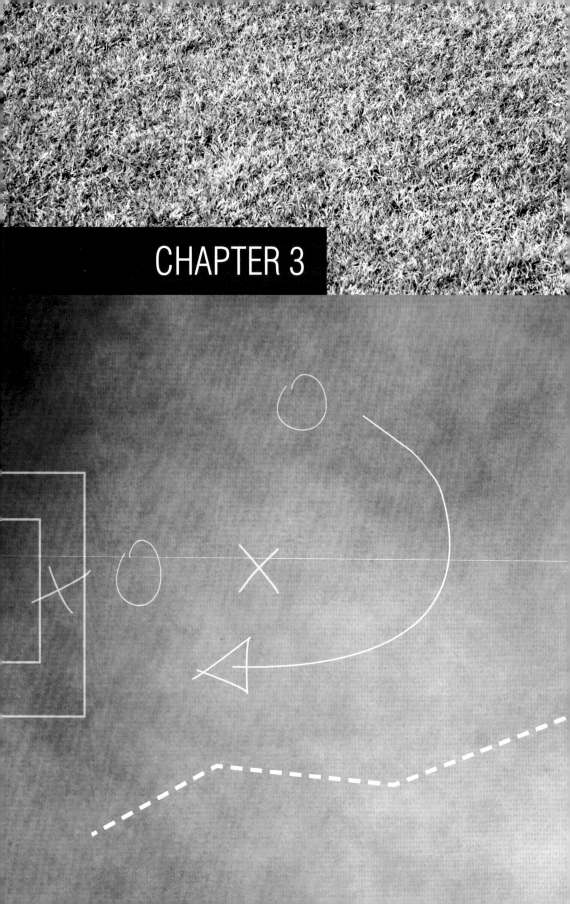

CHAPTER 3

Planning and directing training—Definitions and fundamentals

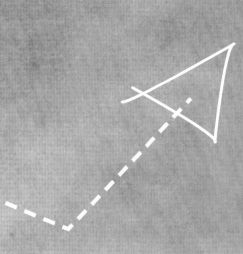

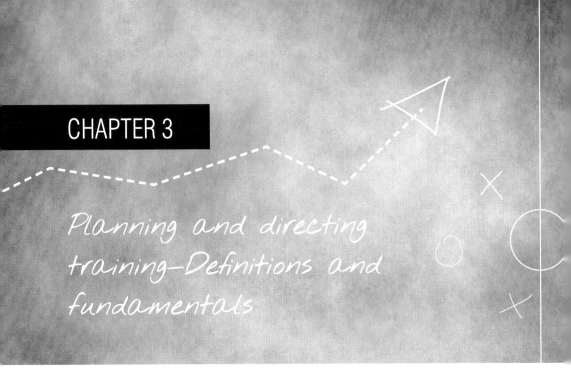

CHAPTER 3

Planning and directing training—Definitions and fundamentals

"I love soccer. I like to play soccer, I like to watch soccer, and I like to talk about soccer. I will barricade myself at Säbener Street and learn everything I need to know about the club, about the Kaderschmiede [youth academy], and especially about the opposition in the Bundesliga."

Pep Guardiola at his first press conference as new head coach for Bayern Munich

*B*efore we take a more in depth look at different periodization models, we must first define and internalize some of the training theory terminology as this will form the basis for subsequent understanding.

3.1 PRINCIPLES OF TRAINING AS THE BASIS FOR ATHLETIC SUCCESS

Following is a brief summary of the most important training principles with interdisciplinary application—including soccer—that every coach should know.

Training

The definition of training is regular and purposeful physical loading to improve performance.

> This implies that any coach who doesn't regularly and purposefully plan does not conduct actual training, but merely an athletic activity.

The law of specificity: It is okay as a regenerative measure in the area of pro sports, but otherwise, cross-country running should be prohibited in soccer. Or does a long-distance runner prepare for competition by playing soccer?

- **The law of specificity**

Specific stimuli trigger specific adaptation reactions.

- **Supercompensation**

There is a dynamic equilibrium (homeostasis) between the body's load requirement and performance level. The adaptation process triggered by training stimuli improves the performance level beyond the starting level (supercompensation).

- **All-or-none law**

Adaptation reactions are triggered only when a critical stimulation threshold is passed.

- **Progression of performance development**

As the performance level increases, the increase in performance continues to diminish despite the increased training effort.

- **Reinforcement of adaptation**

A performance level that has been built up over a longer period of time is considerably more stable than one that is built over a shorter period of time.

- **Trainability and capacity**

Trainability and capacity are subject to age and gender.

Mark Verstegen, fitness coach for the German national soccer team

"Don't train muscles, train movements."

3.2 PRINCIPLES OF TRAINING AS THE BASIS FOR PLANNING AND DIRECTING

"When we win, we always play soccer on Sunday. When we lose, we go for a cross-country run. That's why we always try to win." Kevin Kurànyi—52 international appearances, 19 goals for Germany

The following principles form the basic knowledge for all athletic training:

- **The effective training stimulus principle**

A training stimulus can only trigger an adaptive response if the load components are coordinated so the load dosage exceeds the stimulus threshold.

- **The progressive overload principle**

With an increase in the performance level, the load must be increased to trigger an additional performance increase.

- **The optimal work–recovery ratio principle**

An optimal performance increase is only achieved when the new workload takes place at the highest point of supercompensation.

- **The incomplete recovery principle**

Fatigue due to repeated training stimuli during the recovery phase results in increased supercompensation.

- **The varying training load principle**

Multiple performance factors can be improved simultaneously by varying the training load and alternating the loading of individual subsystems.

- **The right training load structure principle**

Developing a specific fitness-related ability requires a specific composition of the training load structure.

- **The general and specific training principle**

An increasingly specific training is only meaningful when it is based on varied general physical training.

- **The individuality and developmental appropriateness principle**

Individual predisposition and development must be taken into account for optimal performance development.

3.3   PRINCIPLES OF ADAPTATION REINFORCEMENT

"Is the team this good in spite of or because of the coach?"

The long-term training design principle

A stable and high performance level can only be achieved through long-term training design with basic, advanced, and high-performance training.

- **Periodization principle**

An intensive training load period must be followed by a recovery phase because the peak performance cannot be maintained over an entire season.

3.4   TAPERING—ACHIEVING PERFORMANCE AT THE RIGHT MOMENT

Another important term that is particularly important in the area of performance is *tapering*.

Tapering means reduction.

Tapering refers to the reduction in the training load on the days leading up to an important competition phase, such as a world championship. The goal is to reduce the mental and physical stress of daily training, thereby optimizing performance. Depending on the sport, an optimal tapering phase can achieve a 0.5 to 6% performance increase. Thus, the purpose of tapering is to achieve the best possible performance at just the right moment.

When an athlete trains more and harder, he will, on the one hand, become better and stronger, but, on the other hand, he will require more recovery. This is why it is important to create an optimal balance between training load and regeneration. According to Louis Heyer, an optimal training schedule to achieve the maximum performance capacity on competition day is comprised of three phases: normal training, overreaching, and tapering.

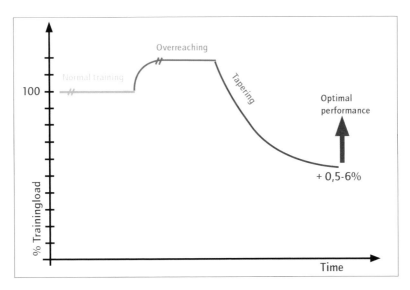

The three phases of training (diagram from Beat Müller/Louis Heyer)

A phase of normal training is followed by the *overreaching* phase with increased intensity (15-20 days) before the volume is reduced during the *tapering* phase.

Here timing is critical:

Taking athletes to the point of optimal performance requires optimal structuring and planning of the tapering phase.

- If the volume is reduced too quickly, the necessary stimulus is no longer great enough.

- If the volume is reduced too slowly, sufficient recovery does not take place, and the performance cannot be achieved in the best possible physical condition.

IT IS IMPORTANT THAT THE INTENSITY IS MAINTAINED (OR EVEN SLIGHTLY INCREASED) IN SPITE OF THE REDUCED VOLUME (UP TO 50% LESS), AND THE FREQUENCY OF TRAINING UNITS IS NOT REDUCED BY MORE THAN 20%.

The progression of tapering is always exponential, meaning the volume is decreased by fixed percentages.

The performance increase that takes place can be explained by the reduction in the training load through tapering subsequent to an overreaching phase, resulting in positive adaptation on a physical (i.e., increased blood volume) and mental (i.e., less fatigue and better sleep quality) level.

Two processes impact the performance:
The training during overreaching increases the potential performance capacity over a certain amount of time, but simultaneously it causes increased fatigue.

Over time, these two effects are then reduced. The fatigue effect is greater but of shorter duration (approximately one-third of the time).

Peak condition is achieved only when fatigue has been greatly reduced and the performance capacity is still sufficiently high.

SOURCE: LOUIS HEYER, RESEARCH ASSOCIATE "SPORT SCIENCE – TRACK & FIELD," BASPO

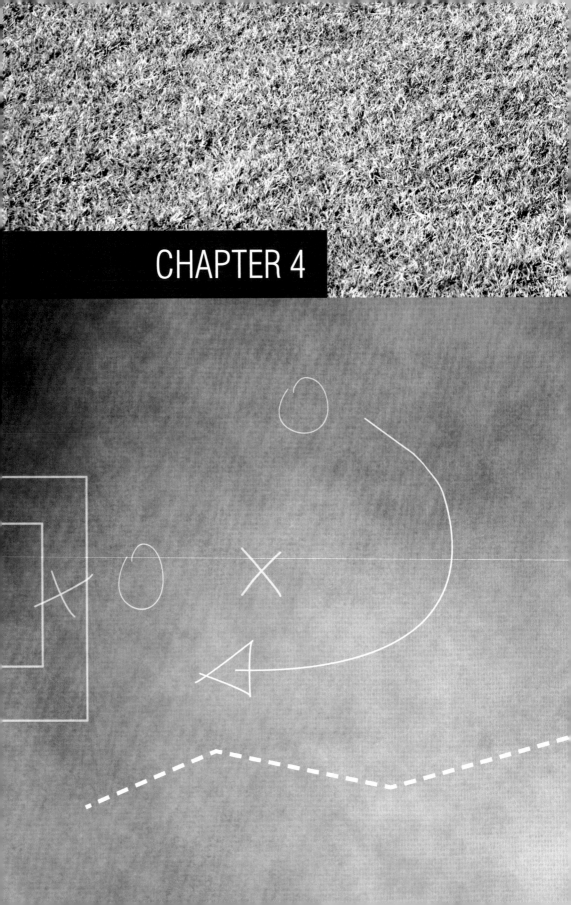

CHAPTER 4

Long-term athlete development—The seven steps of long-term athlete development (LTAD)

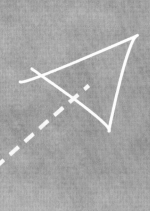

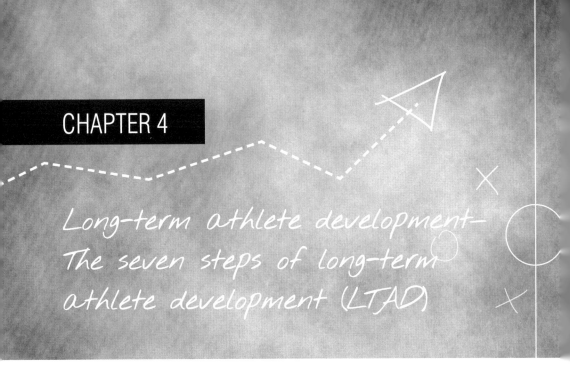

Long-term athlete development— The seven steps of long-term athlete development (LTAD)

"I cannot magically change behavior. It must be trained. And when I say trained, I mean training units."

José Mourinho

To start, every coach must have a clear image of what long-term athlete development should look like.

One of the currently top-rated models representing long-term development is the **long-term athlete development**, or **LTAD**.

LTAD is the brainchild of sport scientist, Dr. Istvan Balyi, one of the world's leaders in long-term athlete development.

Dr. Balyi focuses on an athlete's individual pace of development.

His model is based on seven steps that can be modified and used in recreational and top competitive sports, as well as physical activity in advanced age.

First, the young athlete acquires basic skills based on this model, such as coordination, and then, step by step, the training becomes more performance oriented and sport specific.

According to Dr. Balyi, children learn best when they are having fun, and with ball sports such as soccer, specialization is optimal starting at age 11.

Top youth sports academies such as Ajax Amsterdam, for instance, offer judo training for their young soccer players in an effort to provide integrated training for children.

LTAD according to Dr. Istvan Balyi

One point of criticism Dr. Balyi expresses is that athletes become focused on one sport too soon, meaning their training is too one-sided, and the monotony often causes them to lose enjoyment and also keeps them from developing into a versatile athlete.

That is why the LATD model only starts competitive training at age 16. Prior to that, the athlete should focus on improving sport-specific skills.

The difficult phase of puberty, in particular, must be accompanied by the right steps, because this phase often determines whether an athlete makes it to the top or completely withdraws from competitive sports.

To Dr. Istvan Balyi, it is important that the athlete is seen as a human being, and a holistic view of the athlete is a priority. This is why this model is one of the few, if not the only, models that advocates for long-term athlete development where the age range theoretically starts at birth and ends with death.

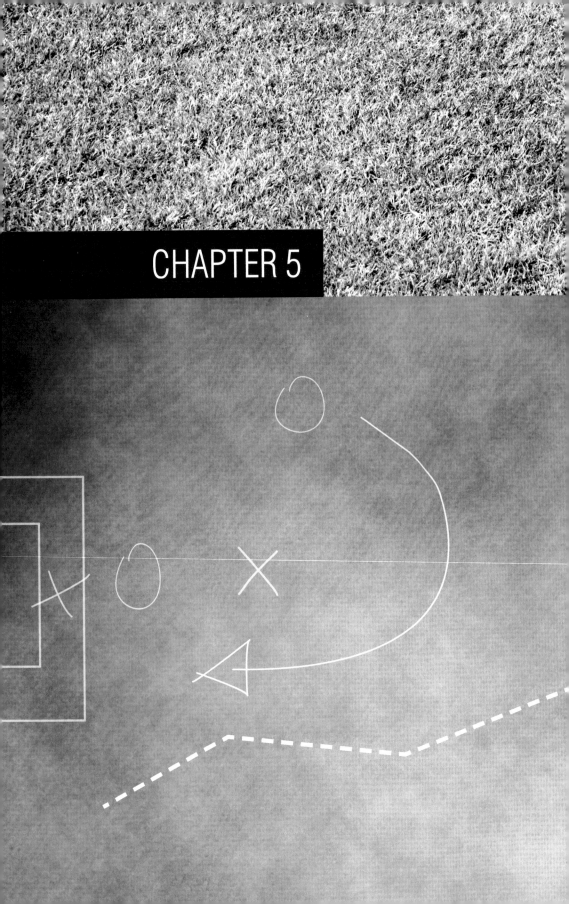

CHAPTER 5

A cross-section of different periodization models

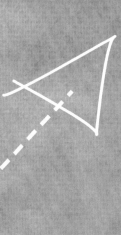

CHAPTER 5

A cross-section of different periodization models

"Just like any other person who has to deal with lots of pressure, a soccer player has what I call 'temor éscenico,' the fear of failure. And how can I neutralize this fear? By automating. By having the player do something he knows, something he practices over and over again, and therefore makes few mistakes."

To increase and maintain performance as well as plan precisely timed peak performances in sports, it is important to closely coordinate recovery phases and changes in the training load.Um diese Höchstleistungen im Sport zu planen, bedarf es einer sogenannten *Periodisierung*.

Planning these peak performances in sports requires periodization.

Periodization is defined as follows:

Periodization is the specification of a continuous series of periods called periodic cycles, with the goal of achieving the best possible performance at a desired point within a training year.

Periodization can be used to establish framework in which planning for performance development in sports occurs.

This is critically important since the human body is not capable of continuously achieving peak performances throughout the year.

In the following chapters, we will first introduce the most common periodization models in sports overall that are also used in soccer, as well as the best known soccer-specific models for the planning and development of training in soccer:

- Classic linear periodization
- Block periodization
- Wave-like periodization
- Coerver Method
- Simon Clifford's Brazilian Soccer Schools
- Horst Wein development model
- Dr. Raymond Verheijen's soccer-specific training model

5.1   CLASSIC LINEAR PERIODIZATION

"In training it isn't necessarily the time you put in that matters, but rather what you accomplish."
– NHL pro Eric Lindros, world-class ice hockey player

Once a long-term development model has been chosen, the long-term phases must be further broken down by periodizing these phases into smaller and smaller units.

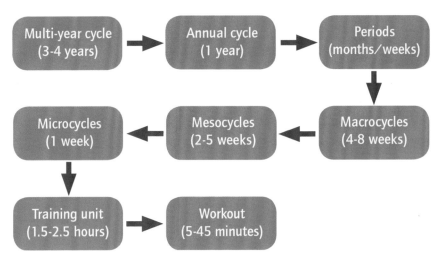

Breakdown of a long-term training structure

Lew Matwejew, a psychologist from the former Soviet Union, is considered the founder of athletic training and classic periodization because he closely analyzed the Soviet Olympic teams of 1952 and 1956, and based on these findings, developed training plans for the 1960 Olympics, where the athletes were able to celebrate great success due to his methods.

Classic periodization is also referred to as linear periodization, and the training method used in classic periodization remains the same throughout an entire mesocycle. Here, the individual areas of performance are trained separately until the desired training goal in one of these areas has been reached.

In classic periodization, an annual plan is created first, regardless of the type of sport.

For Olympic athletes, a quadrennial, meaning a four-year plan, is usually created.

First, it is determined at which competitions, tournaments, or games the athlete or team must bring his or their peak performance.

Practice times for classic periodization in sports with long seasons, such as soccer, must be lowered since there is a match nearly every weekend at which a top performance must be achieved.

In soccer, building on his knowledge as coach for Dynamo Kiev, Walerij Lobanovskyi developed the first periodization versions for soccer based on this periodization concept in the mid-70s and became an eight-time Soviet Champion with his team.

Successful with his long-term planning—Walerij Lobanovskyi of Dynamo Kiev

In this model, the ultimate objective is an athlete's or team's preparation for competition.

Beginning with previously set competition dates, the annual training is rolled up back to front, meaning planning and organizing is done temporally backwards.

Thus, the question is, what must the athlete or team do to achieve the best possible performance on day X, Y, or Z?

In classic periodization, training is planned in such a way that certain factors are trained during specific time periods over the course of the year, while other factors are merely maintained during that time period.

To simplify, the annual plan in most sports, including soccer, is still basically divided into three large blocks:

> Preparation period
> Competition period
> Transition period

Since the season in most soccer leagues includes a preliminary round and a second half, the competition phase can, furthermore, be subdivided into two periods, whereby we then refer to a *double periodization*.

PP = Preparation period

CP = Competition period

TP = Transition period

5.1.1 PREPARATION PERIOD

Some coaches differentiate between a general preparation period in which foundations for physical fitness are created and an advanced period in which *specificity* increases.

Intensity increases until the first high point, which, in soccer, is the first championship game, while the volume simultaneously decreases.

With respect to the first championship game, training becomes increasingly competition specific (see chapter 3.4, Tapering).

But in soccer, a common myth is that the basic endurance established during the general preparation period will last the entire season, which is simply physiologically impossible and is the reason why the general preparation period is, fortunately, gradually disappearing from soccer.

5.1.2 COMPETITION PERIODS

During the *competition period*, the objective is to keep the performance constant or, ideally, to keep improving.

A big mistake often made in soccer is that too little consideration is given to regeneration.

Regeneration is as much a part of the training plan as all the other components:

100% training and 100% regeneration.

It must be an important goal for a coach to have the largest number of players from his squad available for the long haul to maintain a high degree of quality of training and have lots of choices for game day.

In competitive sports, every detail matters:
For a recreational athlete to improve by 5%, he must train about three months. A world-class athlete must train for about two years for a mere 2% improvement.

Next to an optimal diet and the right sleep behavior and massages and saunas, top teams like Bayer Leverkusen or Chelsea FC now are increasingly betting on *cold chambers* that speed up regeneration at -166 °F.

In a cold chamber, all of the vessels directly below the skin are constricted, the blood is forced back, and the body now has more time to optimally supply the working muscles.

When a top athlete uses a cold chamber directly before training or a competition, he afterwards has more explosive power and is able to train approximately 10% longer at the anaerobic threshold.

Is it any wonder that Cristiano Ronaldo had a cold chamber installed in his home?

Law of specificity: Does Usain Bolt do his speed training on the soccer field? No! Then why do so many soccer players spend so much time on the tartan track or trail running?

5.1.3   TRANSITION PERIOD

The competition period is followed by the transition period.

The transition period should be active, but, of course, with a reduced volume and reduced intensity so body and mind can recover.

In the transition period, the players usually complete individual programs that can enhance strengths and eliminate weaknesses.

In addition, classic periodization works with the already proven basis of cyclization.

This cyclization results in three different cycles that build on each other to transition to a more detailed training plan.

> **Microcycle**
   (1-14 days, usually one week of soccer)

> **Mesocycle**
   (2 weeks to 6 months, usually four weeks of soccer)

> **Macrocycle**
   (1-4 years, usually one whole season of soccer)

5.1.4   YEAR-ROUND PERIODIZATION IN SOCCER—DOUBLE PERIODIZATION WITH CYCLIZATION

It has been scientifically proven that *double periodization* is far more advantageous, which is why many teams that use classic periodization in soccer are using double periodization.

With respect to performance, the soccer season usually extends over 11 months and is characterized by the milestones, such as the start of the season, individual match days, or international matches.

The objective here is to stabilize form for the entire season.

To do so, it is important to introduce new stimuli no later than every six to eight weeks to prevent stagnation.

MACROCYCLE I					
Preparation I	Mesocycle I		Mesocycle II		Transition phase I
JUL	AUG	SEP	OCT	NOV	DEC/JAN

MACROCYCLE II					
Preparation II	Mesocycle III		Mesocycle IV		Transition phase II
JAN	FEB	MAR	APR	MAY	JUN

5.1.5   APPLYING CLASSIC PERIODIZATION IN SOCCER

Running in circles around the field is a waste of time and should be prohibited, especially in youth soccer. Instead, a technical and tactical warm-up should be used.

Classic periodization certainly is the basis for considering the planning and directing of an athletic team's training, and even today, every training plan includes the terms preparation period, competition period, and transition period coined by Matwejew.

But, except for the adopted terminology, classic periodization is of little use in soccer as shown by the following:

- The classic periodization model was developed in the 1960s and, to date, is nearly unchanged.
- The model was only tested in individual sports, such as weight lifting and swimming, where there were few high points over the course of the year and for which Matwejew foresaw a five- to six-month preparation period, a four- to five-month competition period, and a brief transition period of one to two months.
- Moreover, for most individual athletes, the high point is the Olympic Games, which only take place every four years.
- But in soccer, there is a high point nearly every weekend, and the timespan for preparation is also considerably shorter.
- Classic periodization focuses on a game density of 10 to 20 competitions, but top international players like Cristiano Ronaldo play more than 70 games during a season.
- The assumption that general fitness training during the preparation phase will be retained for an entire season and disregarded during the competition period does not apply in soccer.
- According to this model, training during the season is of a technical and tactical nature, and target-oriented fitness training is dispensed with, which is absolutely inappropriate for soccer.
- In addition, Matwejew's periodization model was developed in the politically and climatically difficult conditions of the former Soviet Union, with long and extremely cold winters and poorly heated stadiums. This is why this model also developed from the local conditions—a fact that is often forgotten.

5.2   BLOCK PERIODIZATION

"If there is no wind, paddle!"

Verchoshanskij, one of the critics of classic periodization, was instrumental in the development of the *block periodization* model in which emphasis is placed on different aspects over a period of 6 to 12 weeks, but without discontinuing other training content.

Unlike classic periodization, training content in block periodization is not only grouped chronologically but also grouped by the skills necessary for a particular type of sport

MESOCYCLE I			MESOCYCLE II			MESOCYCLE III			MESOCYCLE I			MESOCYCLE II			MESOCYCLE III		
Blocks																	
EP	S	I	R	EP	S	I	R	EP	S	I	R	EP	S	I	R	EP	S	I	R	EP	S	I	R

Simplified depiction of a block periodization

LEGEND		
EP	=	Explosive power
S	=	Speed
I	=	Intermittent
R	=	Recovery

The mesocycles, for instance, are divided into four-week rhythms, and these four weeks are then divided into blocks with different focus areas.

Proponents of block periodization, such as Verchoshanskij or Issurin, expected their approach to result in a higher performance adaptation.

Many world-famous Olympic champions, such as swimmer Alexander Popov or pole-vaulter Sergey Bubka, trained according to the block periodization model.

Olympic champion and six-time world champion: Pole-vaulter Sergej Bubka, one of the best athletes of all time, trained with block periodization

But very good fundamentals on which training can be built are important for this type of periodization.

Block periodization works on training goals sequentially, whereby focus areas are set up in blocks.

Instead of covering different goals and intensities in one cycle, they are spread out over different blocks.

The former block periodization proponents thought that classic periodization would mix too many training concepts, and the mixed training would create mixed results.

It was assumed that the body rapidly adapts to the respective processes, whereby, because of monotonous training, the effectiveness would also leave something to be desired.

Block periodization frequently varies not only the intensity but also the volume to prevent training monotony.

Advances in science and research results have shown that, for instance, the effects of aerobic endurance training can last approximately 30 days, while the effectiveness of speed training already decreases after just a few days—a fact that must be taken into account during planning.

As a consequence, shorter training blocks were developed, which allowed fitness to increase considerably faster.

5.2.1 CHARACTERISTICS OF BLOCK PERIODIZATION

"Some soccer academies are only concerned with winning. We are concerned with training."

World champion, Xavi Hernandez, regarding La Masia, FC Barcelona's soccer school

- The stimuli to develop different motor skills are strung together in a system in which they can build on each other, while the stimuli in the classic periodization model are mixed together.
- In spite of a primary focus area, other training concepts are not neglected.
- Training units possess a high degree of focus and intensity.
- Individual blocks contain a minimal number of training concepts.
- The ATR-model often used for this type of periodization divides block training into a building phase (accumulation): 12 to 30 days for fundamentals; a transition phase (transmutation): 12 to 25 days to develop specific skills; and an implementation phase (realization): 8 to 15 days to maximize performance.
- A significant variation from classic periodization is the quality of training: Classic periodization values volume over intensity, while block periodization puts intensity ahead of volume.

- Since block periodization does not feature parallel training, but rather training that builds on itself, the intensity of the units can be increased.

- Moreover, with the individual blocks, regeneration phases can be easily controlled, which has a positive effect on the athlete's performance level.

5.2.2 USING BLOCK PERIODIZATION IN SOCCER

"That is insane! There are players on the team who run even less that I do!"

Technically brilliant and "genius runner," Toni Polster, Europe's top scorer of 1987, was never a fan of non-sport-specific periodization models.

Block periodization is a progression of classic periodization, providing some useful approaches in soccer, and is used, for instance, by the German Soccer Association—if not for fitness purposes, then for tactical and technical periodization of the German Soccer Association's support program.

But even block periodization is not suitable for integral planning that reflects the complexity of soccer:

- Like classic periodization, block periodization also developed from research and collaboration with individual sports.

- It is impossible to incorporate the game's complexity into this model since the aim of block periodization is not to blend too many training goals, which is not suitable for a multifunctional sport like soccer.

5.3   WAVE-LIKE PERIODIZATION

„Wenn ich auf den Sportplatz ging, suchte ich mir nie die besten Spieler aus. Ich wählte die weniger talentierten Jungen, die bereit waren, hart zu arbeiten, und die gut werden wollten."

These days, many pro soccer players play more than 70 games during an annual cycle, and even elite youth players already play as many as 50 to 60 games in a season.

For this reason, training time must be considerably reduced and its structure must be sport-specific, which is difficult to do with strictly classic periodization and evolved block periodization.

Taking the knowledge from both models of classic periodization and block periodization, Tschiene was one of the first to develop the *wave-like periodization*, or *non-linear periodization*, in 1985.

Proponents of wave-like periodization believe that after two weeks with the same training plan and content only very few adaptation phenomena occur, which significantly reduces the desired output.

Wave-like periodization is a model of training methods that are systematically varied from one training unit to the next, which is a very interesting approach for soccer since nearly every weekend requires an optimal performance. Consequently, the week can be periodized from game to game.

In wave-like periodization, volume, intensity, and number of training units can be used to make adjustments.

This allows training to be more variable, and the quality does not suffer when training units are increased, which is also very helpful in soccer.

To ensure that all of the skills a soccer player needs are at his disposal for the entire season, these necessary skills must be taken into consideration each week at practice.

The body and especially the mind constantly receive new stimuli, which is even more important in game sports than individual sports.

The higher the level, the more important the mind becomes, because it is not challenged nearly as much by classic and block periodization as it is by wave-like periodization.

5.3.1 USING WAVE-LIKE PERIODIZATION IN SOCCER

"Success is not coincidental. It is hard work, persistence, learning, studying, sacrifice, but most of all love for what you are doing or learning."

Pelé, soccer player of the century

Wave-like periodization has some interesting benefits to offer for soccer.

While this model was also derived from individual sports, wave-like periodization makes it possible for the first time to combine different performance factors in soccer training.

- The difference in intensity between the preparation and competitive periods is now considerably lower than with previous models.
- The frequent peaks occurring in soccer are incorporated into this model.
- Overloading and injuries decrease.
- This type of periodization challenges the mind considerably more.
- Wave-like periodization can make soccer training more realistic.

5.4   THE COERVER METHOD

"Watching one time is better than listening a thousand times." – Legendary coach, Wiel Coerver, in action

Many soccer coaches and players are not aware of the enormous impact and, at the time, brilliant ideas of the Dutchman Wiel Coerver.

Wiel Coerver is also referred to as soccer's Albert Einstein.

Wiel Coerver was born on December 3, 1924, in Kerkrade, Netherlands.

Not only did he give his name to the Coerver Method, but he was also one of the groundbreaking coaches in modern soccer, and his ideas were years ahead of their time.

Many practice drills still used in soccer today build on Wiel Coerver's drills or are even borrowed in their entirely. Often, the coaches are aware that they are using Wiel Coerver's drills.

Coerver played pro soccer for Rapid JC, today's Roda JC Kerkrade, and also won the Netherlands national championship in 1956 with this club.

Three years later, Coerver began his coaching career and, in 1974, was able to not only win the national championship but also the UEFA Cup with Feyenoord Rotterdam.

The same year, some of the players from his team lost to Germany in the 1974 World Cup final.

Along with Sparta, Rotterdam, and Go Ahead Eagles, he also worked for Roda JC Kerkrade, where he used to play.

He became world famous with the Coerver Coaching training method, also named after him.

Next to Zeister Vision the Coerver Method is one of the two major training methods in the Netherlands, who doubtlessly is among the leading soccer nations.

The Zeister Vision concept is more in line with street soccer, whereby player development is expedited using the implicit learning approach.

Nevertheless, next to optimal soccer, the Zeister Vision also relies on lots of repetition and good coaching.

Back then, Wiel Coerver did it in a new way and his way.

"Look at the best, learn from the best, be the best."

Wiel Coerver developed his training methods in the 1970s when he noticed that the players' individual quality of play kept diminishing and the training methods in those days did not ensure improvement of individual players.

At the same time, people come to the stadiums to watch breathtaking dribbling à la Maradona or the flashes of genius of a Johan Cruyff.

According to Wiel Coerver, all world-class players have two things in common:

• World-class players are extremely strong in a 1-on-1.

• World-class players are great personalities.

Thus, the Coerver Method's main objective is that soccer players practice the skills of world-class players and grow into great personalities.

For that reason, Wiel Coerver worked for years analyzing the movements and behavior of superstars and broke them down into different levels of difficulty, and based on the results, he then developed training programs for various age and developmental groups.

According to Wiel Coerver, a player must first be perfect in a 1-on-1 before he can practice group and team tactical actions.

In 1983, Wiel Coerver met the two soccer coaches, Alfred Galustian and Charlie Cook, who were immediately enthusiastic about his methods, and together they developed the Coerver Method, which quickly spread around the world through classes, books, DVDs, and other instructional material.

More information and instructional material can be found at

www.coerver.com

5.4.1   THE COERVER PYRAMID METHOD

The Coerver Method divides the main aspects of soccer hierarchically into a pyramid with six levels, which was first illustrated in 1997 as follows:

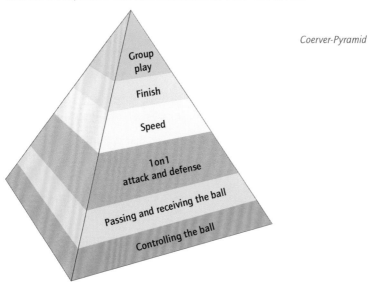

Coerver-Pyramid

It is important to know that the individual contents are not practiced completely separately, as is often claimed, but rather in interesting sequences that build on each other.

Each individual level of the pyramid first teaches the basics, with a subsequent increase in complexity.

Many drills and training concepts are developed in collaboration with the following top European clubs:

- Bayern Munich
- Manchester United
- PSV Eindhoven
- Newcastle United
- Arsenal FC
- FC Nuremberg

World-class with the Coerver Method: Coerver student Meulensteen with his charge, Wayne Rooney

Level 1: Ball control

The first level is all about controlling the ball with both feet because, according to Wiel Coerver, that is the foundation for all other levels.

The player must get to know the ball and make it his best friend by using specially developed movement patterns.

But juggling and controlling the ball also play an important role in developing a feel for the ball and for distances.

The following levels use these movement patterns primarily in the warm-up.

Level 2: Passing and receiving the ball

The second level focuses on passing play and techniques for receiving and controlling the ball, as well as initial group tactical elements.

No other technical element in soccer is used as much as the pass.

Important items at this level:

- Which techniques are used for passing?
- How and where to make contact with the ball?
- When to play which pass?
- When and how is the best way to receive the ball?
- And all of the above when using two-footed training.

Level 3: 1-on-1 attack and defense

The third level of the Coerver Pyramid focuses on 1-on-1 for attack and defense.

- Feints and tricks of the superstars (which are constantly updated and adapted)
- Defensive techniques
- Offensive duels
- Defensive duels
- Courage
- Self-confidence

This level is most certainly the one that most people associate with the Coerver Method.

The coaches' training is also emphasized here, and every Coerver coach is specifically instructed on how to use feints and which details to pay attention to when doing so.

Coerver coaches must also be able to demonstrate the movements themselves based on the motto:

"Watching one time is better than listening one thousand times."

This level first teaches the basics through preliminary exercises and then gradually adds complexity with a perfectly coordinated build-up, all the way to a realistic 1-on-1 under 100% pressure of time and space.

That the Coerver Method is much more than strictly a soccer academy, as is often falsely alleged, can be seen by virtue of the fact that old books about the Coerver Method that were still largely authored by Wiel Coerver himself contain many drills and information regarding defensive techniques, such as the various types of **tackles**, which is nearly completely neglected in other soccer literature.

Sayings like, "He who straddles, loses," unfortunately do not correspond to reality.

When watching pro soccer, one can see world-class players like the currently greatest tackling player in the world, Sergio Ramos, make several tackles during each game. .

The world's greatest tackler in action—world champion and captain of Real Madrid, Sergio Ramos

It is certainly better for a player to run down the opposing player, but when Cristiano Ronaldo or Gareth Gale comes charging with the ball at his feet, a tackle is surely better than an opposing goal

Level 4: Speed

The Coerver Method does not simply focus on running speed but rather the understanding of the speed factor in all its complexity in a realistic setting.

Here, speed training is primarily done in duel form and places great emphasis on action speed and quick perception.

Moreover, Wiel Coerver already made suggestions on jumping to improve explosive power back in the 1980s, which are still cutting edge today.

Level 5: Finish

The fifth level focuses on scoring, scoring, scoring.

Here, the initial focus is on learning the basics of different finishing techniques, such as a clean instep shot, a hip-turn kick, a header, or a bicycle kick.

Subsequently, elements from previous levels are used in goal-scoring combinations.

This is done using preliminary exercises as well as semi-active and 100% duels.

Level 6: Group play

The highest level of the Coerver Pyramid teaches players group tactical forms of play where previously learned concepts are now implemented in a group setting.

According to Coerver, a team's level of play is the sum of its individual levels.

Results from the highest playing level in world soccer, where players such as Lionel Messi, Manuel Neuer, or Cristiano Ronaldo make the difference and determine the outcome of games, confirm the validity of this approach.

Group tactics form the highest level because, according to Wiel Coerver, a soccer game is a succession of individual and group tactical elements in which only groups of players participate before the ball changes location to another group configuration.

During the individual levels of the Coerver Pyramid, players first practice many elements based on the explicit learning approach in which players receive detailed explanations of movements, and the players then copy these movements.

This point, in particular, is often criticized, but when using the implicit learning approach, the technique must also first be practiced explicitly. Anything else is wishful thinking.

The Coerver Method subsequently uses the implicit learning approach, which is why this critique is completely unjustified.

One fantastic approach from the Coerver Method is the previously mentioned positive pushing in which the students receive much praise along with purely constructive criticism, raising their self-confidence.

According to Coach Ricardo Moniz, one of Wiel Coerver's personal students and arguably one of the top technical coaches in the world, Wiel Coerver's top priority was the personal development of the players in which positive pushing played an important role.

But the Coerver Method has not only accompanied many world-class soccer players on their career path, but also two of the students that Wiel Coerver personally trained as coaches are now household names in international soccer:

- **René Meulensteen**, who for many years was Alex Ferguson's assistant coach at Manchester United, where he won the Champions League three times and the Premiere League, and subsequently became head coach for Brondby Copenhagen and FC Fulham.

Coerver coach, René Meulensteen, with Alex Ferguson

- **Ricardo Moniz**, who, after stints as technical coach for PSV Eindhoven, Grasshoppers Zurich, Tottenham Spurs, and Hamburg SV, won the Austrian National Championships and Cup as head coach for Red Bull Salzburg, and also worked for Ferencváros Budapest and 1860 Munich.

Along with the Coerver Method, many soccer associations, such as the German Football Association, have also organized their training structures into pyramid form:

One of the world's best technical coaches—Coerver student, Ricardo Moniz, who won the Austrian Championship and Cup as coach for Red Bull Salzburg.

The German Soccer Association's training structure in pyramid form

	TRAINING LEVELS	AGE GROUPS		TRAINING STRUCTURES			
7	High-performance training—stabilization	Top player	FROM AGE 30	National team International club tournaments National league, regional league			7
6	High-performance training—perfection training		AGE 21-29				6
5	Transition training with appropriate training load	Prospects	AGE 19-20 AGE 17-18	Licensed clubs	National teams U 19 U 20 U 21	Highest amateur level	5
4	Beginning specialization training	JUNIORS U 18/U 19 JUNIORS U 16/U 17	AGE 15-18	Advanced training centers Elite soccer schools	National teams U 15 U 16 U 17 U 18	Talent promotion of clubs	4
3	Soccer-specific fundamental training	JUNIORS U 14/U 15 JUNIORS U 12/U 13	AGE 11-14	Advanced training centers	German Soccer Association talent promotion	Youth club soccer	3
2	Technical play versatility instruction	JUNIORS U 10/U 11 JUNIORS U 8/U 9	AGE 7-10	All-around athletic activities and soccer in clubs and school			2
1	Comprehensive movement instruction	BAMBINI AND YOUNGER U 7	AGE 3-6	Exercise and all-around play in clubs, kindergarten, and school			1

Please note: The transitions from level to level are fluid and gender-specific based on current developmental level.

Please note: Overview of the central talent promotion tiers on each level.

Characteristics and goals of the training-level concept

1	The sub-goals of each training level systematically build on each other.
2	Training levels are geared to developmental phases and, therefore, are fluid.
3	The individual stage of development impacts goals, contents, and methods on every level.
4	The optimization of training structures is an ongoing responsibility.

Characteristics and goals of training structures

1	Each training level has a specific function in the training process.
2	Training levels and structures must be geared to each other.
3	Permeability and openness for individual training paths are central quality characteristics.
4	The optimization of training structures is an ongoing responsibility.

5.5 SIMON CLIFFORD'S BRAZILIAN SOCCER SCHOOLS RECIPE FOR SUCCESS

Simon Darcy Clifford, born in Middlesbrough, England, became world famous through his Brazilian Soccer Schools.

Clifford started his career as an elementary school teacher where he also instructed children in soccer and tried to expose them to the techniques of the Brazilian soccer stars, which marked the beginning of a great franchise system of soccer schools around the world.

In 1997, Clifford borrowed £5,000 to travel to Brazil where he talked to world soccer stars like Zico and Rivelino, who showed him how they as well as the children in Brazil learn their incredible techniques.

In 1998, Clifford opened his Brazilian-style soccer school in Leeds, England, where, next to the tricks of the Brazilian soccer stars, he also worked a lot with Futsal, which, at that time was completely unknown in England.

Similar to Wiel Coerver, Clifford analyzed the movements of top players, whereby Clifford focused strictly on Brazilian players and primarily on movements from Futsal, where nearly all of the top players like Neymar or Ronaldinho learned about soccer.

"Futsal is an extremely important way for children to practice their skills on the ball as well as their understanding of the game. I got my feel for the ball and dribbling from Futsal."

Ronaldinho—from Futsal to 2004 and 2005 World Player of the Year

Clifford's new method for technical training spread extremely fast and was highly respected, so Brazilian Soccer Schools not only spread around England, but the entire world: Hong Kong, Nigeria, South Africa, US, Australia, Netherlands, Thailand, Canada, Malaysia, Bermuda, Singapore, Mexico, and Poland.

Brazilian Soccer Schools is now the largest soccer school organization in the world and consistently has an annual participation of more than a million players.

An estimated 1,700 players who trained at a Brazilian Soccer School have made it to the pro level. The most famous of them is the British national team player, Micah Richards.

You can find more information on Simon Clifford's website:
http://www.braziliansoccerschools.com/

Many soccer stars speak out in favor of Clifford's program, such as the national team player Sócrates with 60 international appearances or the Nigerian Olympic champion Jay-Jay Okocha, who says,

"What Simon is doing is fantastic. Normally what you see in other children is just the basics of the game. He is saying that nothing is impossible. If English players can learn the qualities Simon is teaching, then it will be good for the country."

Clifford's philosophy focuses specifically on individual tactics.

To emphasize the importance of individual skills, he compares soccer players to musicians, who must first learn to master their instrument over a period of years to be able to play in an orchestra with other strong individual players.

In addition to their club training, the elite players in his program must complete one hour of individual training on the ball each day.

For this, he initially uses small size 1 and 2 Futsal balls that barely bounce because he believes that this is the best way to develop technique.

Training units vary by age group, but for younger players, they last nearly two hours and are divided as follows:

- One-third individual ball work
- One-third group tactical forms of play, such as passing or shots on goal
- One-third forms of play in which the coaches are asked to interrupt play as little as possible

In 2003, Clifford bought the club Garforth Town AFC with the goal of bringing this club into the FA Premier League in 20 years.

While the club is still far from reaching this goal, Clifford was already able to move up twice, and well-known players, such as Lee Sharpe, Sócrates, and Careca, laced up their soccer shoes one more time for Clifford.

Furthermore, in 2001, Clifford established a program called *SOCATOS*.

In this unique program children can begin to learn soccer at just six months of age. Next to basic ball skills and fitness exercises, parents are also included to work with the children cognitively on numbers, colors, and letters as part of the training. Moreover, Simon Clifford is a strong supporter of individual training units. He did one-on-one coaching with soccer stars, such as Michael Owen, Wayne Rooney, and Theo Walcott, and also made a name for himself as Keira Knightley's technical coach for the soccer movie Bend It Like Beckham.

2001 European Player of the Year, Michael Owen, used the knowledge he gained from Simon Clifford for individual technique training

5.6 THE HORST WEIN DEVELOPMENTAL MODEL

"Without a question it is necessary to do drills that improve technique, but to practice technique outside of a game isn't very useful. The learner needs context."

Horst Wein—his name is closely tied to the term game intelligence in soccer.

When it comes to the topic of *game intelligence* in soccer, it is impossible not to invoke the name Horst Wein. Along with many soccer associations, he has also been an advisor to FC Barcelona. What many don't know is that Horst Wein's original background is field hockey. Born in 1941 in Hannover, Germany (died in February 2016), Horst Wein is a former player on the German national field hockey team, where he made 40 international appearances for the German national team.

In 1969, Horst Wein made the switch to coach for the German national field hockey team.

In 1972, Horst Wein was the director for the hockey tournament at the Munich Olympics, and a year later, he became the coach for the Spanish national field hockey team.

Horst Wein lives near Barcelona, Spain, and one of his two sons, Christian, became European Champion with the German national team in 1999 and 2003 and field hockey world champion in 2002.

To systematically teach his son game intelligence, Wein developed a well-conceived model that has gained much international attention.

In the early 1980s, Horst Wein made the switch to soccer and there continued to develop his training model, which takes into account the type of thinking and playing of street soccer where fewer and fewer players are learning the soccer ABCs. This is why Wein makes the case for bringing street soccer into the clubs. Over the course of his career, Wein has published more than 30 sports books and numerous articles, particularly on the topic of game intelligence in soccer. Additionally, Wein is the author of soccer training DVDs and a technical consultant for hockey software.

Wein's books and DVD's have been published in many languages, such as German, Spanish, English, Dutch, Italian, Japanese, and Russian, and he is a world-renowned top expert in soccer coach training.

His standard work, Developing *Game Intelligence in Soccer*, is a must-have.

The world-famous American sports publisher, Human Kinetics, even calls Horst Wein:

"Perhaps the world's foremost mentor of soccer coaches."

Next to Horst Wein, another well-known man from hockey has also made a name for himself: Bernhard Peters (Olympic champion as coach of the German national field hockey team). After being hired as head coach for youth soccer at TSG 1899 Hoffenheim, he is now in charge of the athletic future of the soccer youth at Hamburg SV.

While soccer training methods initially focused very heavily on *technique* during the first 100 of its roughly 150-year history, in the 1960s, major emphasis was placed on *fitness* until, after the fitness wave in the 1980s, training took on an extremely *tactical* focus. Now soccer finds itself in a phase based on Horst Wein's approach in which improvements are achieved primarily through game intelligence because this aspect has been neglected so far and a great wealth of experience already exists in the other areas.

To Wein, soccer consists of many technical and situations that players must recognize and comprehend. Ideally, a player should be able to draw on an extensive wealth of experience to find the best possible solution.

Moreover, scientific research supports the significance of game intelligence: 60% of all turnovers in soccer result from errors in perception, comprehension, and decision-making.

5.6.1 THOUGHTS ON GAME INTELLIGENCE IN SOCCER

"Don't give your players fish, but show them how to do the fishing."

Everyone in soccer is talking about the term *game intelligence*, regardless of whether the topic is youth soccer training or soccer at the highest level.

In modern soccer, game intelligence is more important than ever since most teams can stand eye to eye on a physical, technical, and tactical level thanks to modern training methods.

For the optimal development of a soccer player, game intelligence must be an inherent part of training from a young age.

The difference in quality between individual players is determined more and more by their degree of game intelligence.

A soccer player benefits little from a superior physical condition or better technique if he is unable to intelligently apply these elements for the good of his team.

According to Horst Wein, in order to have more soccer players with a high degree of game intelligence on the field in the future, soccer coaches must offer their players more stimulation and less instruction.

Playing soccer on the highest level demands an extremely high degree of game intelligence that must be fostered starting at an early age.

Due to the enormous progress in training methods in modern soccer, outstanding technical, tactical, and physical training has become a matter of course for every player.

With game intelligence, there is now another aspect pushing to the fore that often makes the critical difference.

For this reason, the development of game intelligence in soccer training should be given special attention.

When training young soccer players, instead of focusing solely on learning technical and tactical elements, the mind should be trained as well as the muscles and nervous system so that a soccer player is able to tap his full potential.

The more intelligent players are on the field, the more likely the game will be played at a higher level.

Host Wein has the following to say on the subject:

"Game intelligence has nothing to do with the number of neurons in a soccer player's brain but rather the number of connections individual cells can make between each other. To create many of these connections a soccer player must be stimulated often and properly."

This means game intelligence in soccer depends only partly on genetic factors.

Instead, game intelligence in modern soccer must be trained using many suitable drills, to which end Horst Wein has developed specific forms of play and game models.

Furthermore, it is very important to train game intelligence in soccer with forms of open play similar to street soccer.

As with all people, in soccer, a player's intelligence is expressed in different ways.

Each position and task a player has requires a different type of game intelligence, because the problems a goal player must solve are different than those of a forward or central defender.

Children and adolescents learn best by watching. That is why demonstrations by the coach are especially important, because that is how players learn fastest. A coach's ability to demonstrate must, therefore, be highly developed.

The following quote by the Chinese philosopher Confucius highlights an important factor in learning new skills:

I hear and I forget.

I see and I remember.

I do and I understand.

It is scientifically proven that children gather valuable experience by trial and error and practice.

But if a child would have to make due with only his own experiences, he would not be able to achieve a high intellectual level or advanced motor skills.

This requires the experience of adults who help the child reach a higher level through words and demonstrations.

This does not only apply to different learning situations, such as in a family or at school, but also to tactical thinking and behavior on the soccer field.

Elevating the level of play is the responsibility of the soccer coaches. This elevation can only be achieved if training includes games that systematically practice correctly analyzing a game situation as well as correctly solving the game situation mentally and the flawless execution of the planned action.

It is how soccer players acquire the ability to not only read a game situation correctly, but also to correctly anticipate its possible further development based on the assimilated and processed information.

This ability to anticipate is always preceded by an optimal cognitive ability. To be able to take full advantage of this ability requires automating the soccer technique so the player possesses important capacities that allow him to make intelligent and anticipatory decisions without constantly looking at the ball.

Acquiring tactical knowledge and, thus, game intelligence does not only happen through conscious and subconscious action in open play, but often results in conjunction with a goal-directed educational process.

As soon as their technical and tactical ability allows, soccer players should be given the opportunity during these processes to gather tactical knowledge and experience through independent thinking and action that will help them recognize which effect a certain behavior has in a certain game situation.

The more this knowledge is acquired through personal observation, thinking, and experimenting, the deeper it will be.

"The more knowledge a player has, the more he sees." – Horst Wein

This is also a major factor in the strength of players like Xavi and Iniesta who have played hundreds of games at the highest level and, thus, have acquired more and more knowledge and are able to make better and better decisions.

Game intelligence in soccer can be fostered through open play, called *implicit training*, as is common in street soccer, and also through *explicit training*.

Often subjective playing experience alone, the way it is acquired in street soccer, is not enough to cultivate game intelligence.

A goal-directed educational process, called *explicit training*, gives the coach the important task of making the tactical knowledge a player has acquired himself or from someone else visible and deliberate, and after a thorough demonstration, giving a detailed explanation of the same and systematizing it for a better overview.

Elements that take place during a soccer game, such as getting open, passing, taking shots on goal, receiving and controlling the ball, and feinting, should be learned through motor exercises.

A player with game intelligence also knows how to meld these elements and to optimally solve them according to the respective game situation.

When searching for the best possible solution for a game situation, an intelligent player quickly sees the options as well as the dangers.

While he perceives and analyzes the actions of his teammates and opponents, he already knows and has mastered the different solutions to emerging problems and knows how to put them into practice.

This distinguishes a player with a high degree of game intelligence from a player with less game intelligence.

According to Horst Wein, implicit training exercises should also be used in soccer. Only specific instruction and demonstration by the coach as well as a sufficient number of repetitions of the same tactical action in the same game situation and, finally, the application of the identified solution to other similar game situations creates a solid foundation for a high degree of game intelligence.

During implicit game intelligence training, the coach only presents certain parts of the game.

While practicing repeatedly, the players learn which alternative actions to use with the opponent's actions.

5.6.2 GAME INTELLIGENCE DURING COMPETITION

"Soccer is a game that starts in the head, from there goes through the heart, and ends in the feet." – Horst Wein

Following are several examples of what distinguishes a soccer player with a high degree of game intelligence, as per Horst Wein:

- A soccer player with lots of game intelligence is able to make better decisions on the soccer field more quickly.
- He possesses excellent anticipation ability and is, therefore, able to recognize game situations early and judge them accurately.
- He has the ability to read a game situation correctly and compare the game situation to an identical or similar one and, thereby, is able to make the best possible decision.

- A player with lots of game intelligence tries to find an optimal solution to a game situation through tactical thinking and does so creatively.
- An intelligent soccer player is a good team player without neglecting his individual strengths.
- He thinks and acts for his teammates by correctly assessing the situation.
- A player who plays only for himself without contributing his game intelligence to the team will never become a good soccer player because he only sees segments of the game.
- An intelligent player learns from his mistakes and is self-critical.
- He recognizes different opportunities and dangers in a game situation.
- He tries to balance risk and safety. Too much risk, for instance, can result in a turnover.
- Conversely, too much safety keeps a player from bringing his best possible performance.
- An intelligent player is also very calm on the ball, assured in his respective space and game situation, and completely confident because he knows he can provide the optimal solution to the game situation due to his vast experience.
- He also knows that he cannot do everything right, which is why his performance is not negatively affected by mistakes. He knows when it is best to play the ball or when he has to dribble.
- He is able to speed up the game as the situation demands, or, if necessary, to slow it down.
- He wants to continue to improve and plays simple and precise soccer.
- He already knows what his next action will be before he receives the ball.
- Moreover, a player with a high degree of game intelligence is always able to not only adapt to new game situations, but also to his teammates and opponents as well as the referee and external conditions.

5.6.3   DIGRESSION: "I LIKE CONTROLLED CHAOS"—QUICKER PERCEPTION, QUICKER ACTION IN SOCCER AS A MENTAL SPORT

Ralf Rangnick's mentor, Helmut Groß, on the importance of mental training and the high physical demands of modern soccer

To further reinforce the importance of game intelligence, following is a summary of some highly interesting statements from an interview with a coach who, 30 years ago, was one of the first coaches to use zonal defense in the entire German-speaking realm.

The discourse is by Helmut Groß, who currently serves as training advisor as well as being in charge of game philosophy at RB Leipzig and Red Bull Salzburg.

Helmut Groß established the extremely successful youth program at VfB Stuttgart and is father figure and mentor to star coaches like Ralf Rangnick, Thomas Tuchel, and Marcus Sorg, who recently led the German U19 team to the European Championship title.

Helmut Groß is known for his accurate predictions on how soccer will evolve.

In a rare interview, this absolute soccer expert makes the following assertions:

"…I imagine that Guardiola's training includes lots of mental training."

"…at the end of the day, a player must be able to quickly make the right decision under extreme pressure of time or space."

"…things are evolving at a terrific pace. Players must continue to improve. That means primarily quicker cognition, quicker analysis, making the right decision quicker, acting quicker."

"…Brain potential is enormous. We can't even properly estimate that."

"…The biggest growth rates are in mental training…"

"…Barcelona only scouts for talents that meet the athletic requirements along with the coordinative abilities…"

"…in the future, we should focus more on improving cognitive abilities…"

"…a central defender plays in the red zone and must be able to offer resistance, even in the air. That requires strength, good timing, and explosive power…"

And Helmut GroÐ's core statement is: The biggest growth rates in soccer, by far, are in the area of cognition, or as Horst Wein would say, game intelligence!

You can find the complete interview in German with soccer expert Helmut Groß at:

http://www.faz.net/aktuell/sport/fussball/im-gespraech-trainer-helmut-gross-ich-mag-das-kontrollierte-chaos-12342163.html

5.6.4   TRAINING GAME INTELLIGENCE—THE HORST WEIN FIVE-STEP DEVELOPMENTAL MODEL IN DETAIL

"Playing soccer without thinking is like taking a shot on goal without aiming!"

To Horst Wein, soccer is a cognitive percentages game of knowledge—the more a player knows, the better he is.

According to Horst Wein, a soccer player, ideally, should bring the following qualifications to the table:

- He must be fast (stride frequency).
- He must have willpower.
- He must be intelligent.

The eyes as an extension of the brain play an important role because, according to Horst Wein, every action in soccer consists of these four phases:

- **Cognition**
- **Comprehension and interpretation**
- **Decision-making**
- **Technical execution.**

Game intelligence in soccer is trained by practicing drills that simulate the game.

As previously mentioned, according to Horst Wein, the focus should be much more game oriented, and based on his development model, every practice should start with a game.

In doing so, the goal is not only to impart knowledge, but also to prompt the players to properly apply what they have learned.

Knowledge alone accomplishes nothing. Only knowledge that is applied correctly will make a player successful.

Here motor and cognitive learning go hand in hand.

In modern soccer training, technique and game intelligence should always be developed using complex drills.

The coach confronts his players with realistic situations that require the players to make a quick decision and implement it through motor actions.

The development of a young soccer player's game intelligence is subject to the many different stimuli and suggestions he receives during practice and also during competitive play.

Each new stimulus creates a new connection between the many neurons. If the soccer player is alert and extremely motivated at the time of perception and is also interested and confident in his abilities, an optimal starting point for a major learning effect has been created.

Horst Wein's development model consists of a total of five steps and builds on plays that the players initially practice individually and subsequently develop group tactical and team tactical elements built on these plays:

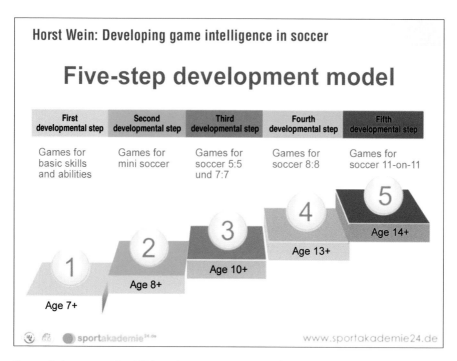

You can find many great Horst Wein products at www.soccer-coaches.com/

First of all, it is important to know that Horst Wein differentiates between two coaching approaches.

The bad approach, where the coach is the center of attention, dictates everything, and puts pressure on the players:

A **good approach** that puts the players at the center, which creates confident, intelligent, and creative players:

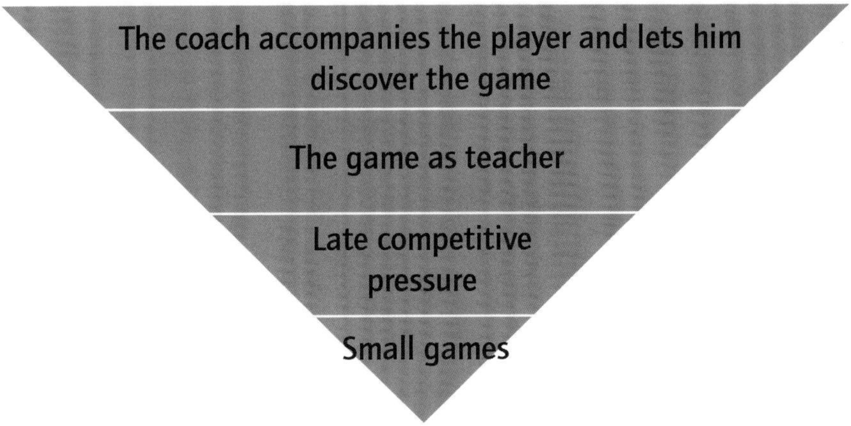

The coach accompanies the player and lets him discover the game

The game as teacher

Late competitive pressure

Small games

Building on this foundation, Horst Wein divides his youth soccer development model into five steps designed to adapt to a child's growth process.

Thus, a soccer player must complete four developmental steps until he reaches the fifth step, which corresponds to an actual game.

The individual steps are characterized by increasing complexity, which forces the players to learn to read the game more and more quickly.

The central question of Horst Wein's development model is:

What is the best way to develop a young soccer player's potential step by step?

First developmental step

DEVELOPING GAME INTELLIGENCE IN SOCCER   SLIDE 3

The soccer development model
Step 1
(For children age 7+)

Games for basic skills and abilities

Ball school	Games for ball control	Games for passing, receiving the ball, shots on goal	Games in a labyrinth	Games for individual defense	Multipurpose games	Triathlon 2-on-2

Soccer decathlon

Second developmental step

DEVELOPING GAME INTELLIGENCE IN SOCCER   SLIDE 4

The soccer development model
Step 2
(For children age 8+)

Games for FUNiño

Games for basic skills and abilities	Playing ability test in FUNiño	Preparatory and correction games for FUNiño	Simplified games 2-on-2 with correction games	Triathlon 3-on-3

FUNiño-Pentathlon

Playing ability in FUNiño 3-on-3

Third developmental step

The soccer development model
Step 3
(For children age 10+)

5-on-5 and 7-on-7 games for soccer

Games for **FUN**iño	Goal player training Goal player decathlon	Simplified games 3-on-3 with correction games	Games for basic skills and abilities	Indoor soccer 5-on-5 (Futsal)	Triathlon 4-on-4

5-on-5 and 7-on-7 soccer playing ability

Fourth developmental step

The soccer development model
Step 4
(For children age 13+)

8-on-8 games for soccer

7-on-7 games for soccer	8-on-8 playing ability test for soccer	Programs for soccer IQ during attacking actions	Simplified games 4-on-4 5-on-5 Correction games	Programs for soccer IQ during defensive actions	Triathlon 6-on-6

8-on-8 soccer playing ability between both penalty areas on a regulation field

Fifth developmental step

The soccer development model
Step 5
(For children age 14+)

Games for an official 11-on-11 game

Games for 8-on-8 soccer	Team and group training to improve defensive and attacking behavior	Individual training depending on weaknesses and player position	Practice of set pieces

11-on-11 soccer playing ability

5.6.5 HORST WEIN'S MINI SOCCER CONCEPT FUNIÑO AND MANCHESTER UNITED'S U9 STUDY

"A pass must be born from necessity." – Horst Wein

In his concept, Horst Wein basically suggests the following numbers of players and ball sizes for different age groups:

U 6 and under	U 7-U 9
• No competition • Play with the ball at home	• Number of players: 3-on-3 • Ball size: 3
U 10	**U 11-U 12**
• Number of players: 5-on-5 • Ball size: 4	• Number of players: 7-on-7 • Ball size: 4
U 13	**U 14 and over**
• Number of players: 8-on-8 • Ball size: 4	• Number of players: 11-on-11 • Ball size: 5

The importance of the small games used by Horst Wein can be seen in the **Manchester United Youth Academy U9 team study: Comparison 8-on-8 vs. 4-on-4**

In a study from 2002-2003 with Manchester United's U9 team, Dr. Rick Fenoglio analyzed video footage of 15 games of 4-on-4 and 15 games of 8-on-8 soccer.

The results clearly speak for themselves and could not be more evident.

Passes played	Over 135% or 585 more passes played in 4-on-4 than 8-on-8
Shots on goal	Over 260% or 481 more shots on goal in 4-on-4 than 8-on-8
Goals scored	Over 500% or 301 more goals scored in 4-on-4 than 8-on-8
1-on-1 situations	Over 225% or 525 more 1-on-1 situations in 4-on-4 than 8-on-8
Feints, tricks, dribbling	Over 280% or 436 more feints, tricks, and dribbling in 4-on-4 than 8-on-8

Additionally, game intelligence in soccer can be easily extrapolated with games that have a technical and tactical emphasis because, in this type of positional play, soccer players always have more alternative solutions in reserve.

Here, the 4-on-4 is the smallest version of the large 11-on-11 where all the possible solutions that are also available in an 11-on-11 are already at their disposal, which makes it the ideal choice for training young soccer players.

Horst Wein wants the players to discover the answers themselves by using open questions. The following illustration shows an explicit drill on the left, and an implicit drill on the right side:

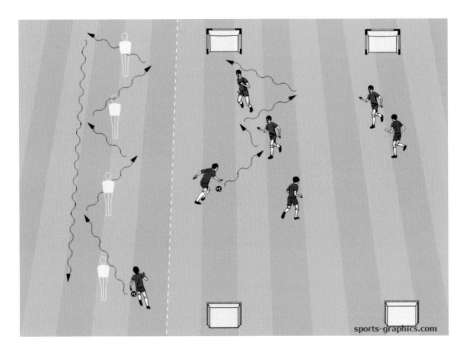

The player on the left dribbles through the slalom course, using feints; the player on the right is "forced" by the choice of play to fake out his opponents, but, in addition, this player must continuously reassess the situation.

According to Horst Wein, this is the only way to truly develop game intelligence.

This systematic approach can be used from practicing without predetermined behavior to practicing with specific predetermined defensive or offensive behavior to open play without any restrictions.

In open play without restrictions, the player must learn from his own experiences which solution among the many alternatives is the best action for which opponent behavior.

It is important to know that it doesn't matter whether a tactical behavior during competitive play originates from a rehearsed behavior or from the soccer player's own creativity as long as the game situation is solved in the best possible way.

Even better from Horst Wein is his invention FUNiño, the basic premise of which is 3-on-3 with four goals.

To Horst Wein, the 2-on-1 in FUNiño plays a particularly important role, because he considers 2-on-1 the atom of the game.

Wein is convinced that games played on four goals that are positioned far apart are better for the development of game intelligence than the game with two central goals because, aside from many other advantages, in this form of play the players must learn to recognize superior number situations from a very early age.

The following are benefits of the **FUNiño** program:

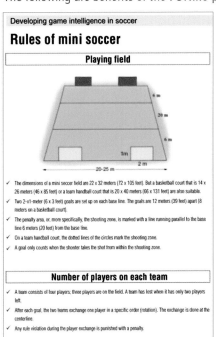

- FUNiño games allow children to discover behaviors that characterize the best players in the world on or off the ball.
- The games allow for more touches.
- FUNiño games give more opportunity to try out techniques.
- They have more offensive options.
- They have more defensive options.
- FUNiño games increase cognition.
- The games allow for more opportunities to solve problems in a game.
- Everyone gets involved; no one can hide.
- They offer more scoring opportunities and more goals.
- FUNiño games offer more fun and playing enjoyment.

5.6.6   EXAMPLES OF OPEN QUESTIONS IN SOCCER

Keeping the ball close to the foot and a perfect overview—world-class player, Xabi Alonso

"An intelligent coach constantly inspires new ideas in his players and allows them to actively learn because his job is to inspire his players to think rather than think for them. To achieve this he must allow them a certain amount of freedom, and by asking the right questions teach them to solve problems themselves and make good decisions." – Horst Wein

Horst Wein Seminar attendees often ask themselves what the important open questions are in the Horst Wein training concept, which is why we have listed the following examples:

- Was that good?
- Would you do that again?
- What could you have done differently?
- When should you lay off the ball?
- How could you prevent this?
- What is the ideal moment for the player in possession to play a pass?
- What is the advantage of superior number situations?
- What is the advantage when you can outplay an opponent?
- Who needs to capture the ball now?
- Which of the two goals is it easier to score a goal on?
- Why do you play the ball to the left instead of the right?
- How should the offensive player attack the player in possession?
- How does the forward best position himself relative to the marking defender in order to keep possession?

5.7   DR. RAYMOND VERHEIJEN'S MODEL

"Soccer fitness comes from playing soccer."

Considered the world's best fitness trainer in soccer —Dr. Raymond Verheijen in conversation with the Dutch national team coach, Guss Hiddink.

Considered the world's best fitness trainer in soccer—Dr. Raymond Verheijen in conversation with the Dutch national team coach, Guss Hiddink

Dr. Raymond Verheijen (born 1971) is considered the world's leading soccer fitness trainer.

Verheijen's top priority is to make soccer training as close to a real game as possible based on the law of specificity.

He is known as a major critic of non-soccer training methods, which he frequently likes to assert with a note of sarcasm on his Twitter account:

https://twitter.com/raymondverheije

David Moyes, coach of Manchester United, was the target of some harsh criticism. Verheijen referred to him as a "dinosaur" and blamed him for the injuries of Verheijen's fellow countryman, Robin van Persie.

In addition, Verheijen published his soccer manual, *Conditioning for Soccer*—highly respected in soccer circles—in 2000, as well as the cutting-edge book, *The Original Guide to Football Periodisation*, in 2014.

So far Verheijen has participated in three World Cups as fitness trainer for the Netherlands, South Korea, and Russia.

It was the South Korean team's extremely running-intensive playing style at the 2002 World Cup—where they took fourth place—that made quite a splash at the time and caused the experts to wonder which methods Verheijen used to get the team in such good shape.

Moreover, Verheijen worked with many top teams, such as FC Barcelona, Chelsea FC, Manchester City FC, and FC Zenit Saint Petersburg.

After a brief stint as national coach for Wales, Verheijen also worked as a personal trainer for top players, such as Craig Bellamy and Bayern Munich star player, Arjen Robben.

Drawing on the knowledge of Dr. Raymond Verheijen—Arjen Robben, the fastest player in the world at 22.9 mph.

Currently, Verheijen travels extensively on behalf of his World Football Academy and holds trainings and lectures around the world:

http://worldfootballacademy.com/

Raymond Verheijen also talks about four performance factors in soccer:
- Communication,
- Game insight (tactics)
- Technique
- Soccer fitness

Based on Verheijen's holistic approach and the law of specificity, these four components should always be practiced in a realistic setting and are closely linked to the four game phases..

Verheijen argues for a standardized "soccer language" and is annoyed by non-soccer fitness trainers in soccer who are unfamiliar with this soccer language. .

Verheijen's concepts are also referred to as the Dutch version of tactical periodization whereby, contrary to tactical periodization, Verheijen does not place any specific emphasis on the four factors.

"The biggest problem in football, with respect to fitness, is the exercises. Fitness is trained as something separate to football."

5.7.1 THE FOUR FITNESS-RELATED ABILITIES AS PER VERHEIJEN

1. **Maximum explosiveness and quality of actions**

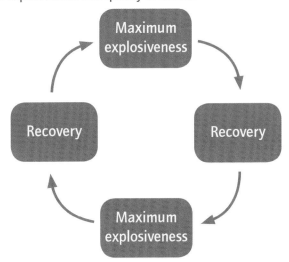

- Is best practiced in a 1-on-1 with a shot on goal because here the soccer players sprint faster and more effectively than during an individual sprint.

2. Quick recovery between two explosive actions

(ME = Maximum explosiveness; R = Recovery)

- Soccer is a serial sprint discipline in which players complete actions with maximum explosiveness again and again and must quickly recover for the next action.

3. **Explosive power endurance**

- Explosive power endurance is necessary to still have the ability to act dynamically at the end of a game and to maintain quality of action.

- Is best trained with sprints and brief breaks with a loading duration of approximately two minutes.

4. **Quick recovery between two explosive actions at the end of a game**

- This refers to maintaining quality throughout the entire game.

- According to Verheijen, this ability is best trained in small games like 4-on-4 plus goal player for one minute to two minutes max.

Verheijen derives drills and plays on the ball from the game for every skill and shows when to practice what in the course of the week, or rather, the season.

There is, maximally, one fitness unit per week, which is referred to as *soccer fitness* and is executed on the ball.

"Everything has to be football related". – (Dr. Raymond Verheijen)

Verheijen always asks coaches if they train their soccer players the traditional way or the correct way.

Traditional:

- Endurance runs as fitness training.
- Injuries due to constant intensive loading.
- Amateurs: lots of running units during the first two to three weeks.
- Pros: Running camp.
- Training load decreases during second half of preparation phase.
- End of championship tournament: workload is reduced because players are exhausted.

Correct:

- Soccer fitness acquired by playing soccer.
- Only one unit of soccer fitness per week.
- Fitness can be trained and optimized by playing throughout the season.
- Based on the same model, fitness is not only maintained, but is incrementally improved over the course of the season.
- Intensive training is also possible at the end of the season.

TRADITIONAL		SOCCER-BASED FITNESS
Medium to high	**Intensity**	Very high
General and soccer-specific	**Fitness goals**	Soccer-specific
Several times a week	**Frequency during preparation**	Once a week
Once a week	**Frequency during season**	Once a week
Wave-like	**In-season periodization**	Increasing
On and off the ball	**On or off the ball?**	On the ball
Concomitant/guided	**Testing/diagnostics**	Not necessary

"For example, first you do a certain exercise on a certain pitch size, and then you make the pitch size smaller. The same exercise but less space, less time, increasing the demands, and that is how you improve players." – Raymond Verheijen

Verheijen, too, periodizes not only the season as well as individual training weeks, but also the types of drills and styles of play used, which he categorizes according to the number of players and the size of the field as well as coaching points into different fitness focus areas:

- 1-on-1/2-on-2
> Soccer sprints: intensive intervals for maximally dynamic actions

- 3-on-3/4-on-4
> Extensive intervals

- 5-on-5/6-on-6/7-on-7
> Intensive endurance

- 8-on-8 to 11-on-11
> Extensive endurance

In this context, it is important to know that from Verheijen's point of view as well as that of current sport science, in soccer, oxygen is not used for the respective actions since those are rarely aerobic, but rather for recovery between individual actions, which should, however, also be trained as realistically as possible and not with endurance runs.

Verheijen's simplified representation of a season is based on the first half of the season as follows:

1	2	3	4	5	6	7	8	9	10	11	12	13	14	15	16	17	18	19	20	21	22	23	24
Preparation 1						Preparation 2						Championship											
Cycle 1						Cycle 2						Cycle 3						Cycle 4					
SF		SF		SF		SF		SF		SF		SF		SF		SF		SF		SF		SF	
11-on-11		7-on-7		4-on-4		11-on-11		7-on-7		4-on-4		11-on-11		7-on-7		4-on-4		11-on-11		7-on-7		4-on-4	
8-on-8		5-on-5		3-on-3		8-on-8		5-on-5		3-on-3		8-on-8		5-on-5		3-on-3		8-on-8		5-on-5		3-on-3	
PFS		PFS		PFS		10 x 15 m per field player																	
80 x		60 x		30 x																			
40 m		30 m		15 m																			

SF = Soccer Fitness; PFS = Playing Field Size

Example of soccer fitness training during cycle 1 built on this season coaching plan:

Week 1	Week 2	Week 3	Week 4	Week 5	Week 6

SF		SF		SF	
11-on-11		7-on-7		4-on-4	
8-on-8		5-on-5		3-on-3	
80 x 40 m		60 x 30 m		30 x 15 m	
4 x		6 x		10 x	
8-10 min		3-4 min		1-2 min	

Sample soccer fitness training structure as per Verheijen:

Warm-up	Technical warm-up on the ball plus running ABCs and acceleration Duration: 15 minutes
Main part	2-on-2 plus two goal players Playing field: 20 x 10 meters Playing time: 1 hour 30 minutes Repetitions: 10
Conclusion	Cool-down run: 20 minutes

Verheijen's model is flexible, and depending on the respective training goal, the drills can be adapted to lower or higher intensities.

All of Verheijen's considerations are based on the motto:

„Quality over quantity."

The second international top man after Verheijen in the area of soccer fitness—former pro player and Champions League winner and now assistant coach for Juventus Torino, Dr. Jens Bangsbo

After Dr. Raymond Verheijen, we must absolutely mention Dr. Jens Bangsbo, who is considered the most eminent international expert on soccer fitness next to Verheijen.

Dr. Jens Bangsbo is credited with the *Yo-Yo intermittent recovery test (YYIRT)*, which measures intermittent recovery, an extremely performance-limiting factor in soccer.

Bangsbo is a highly respected professor at the University of Copenhagen Institute of Exercise and Sport Sciences and author of many books, and he has been very successful in the practical application of his methods.

The former pro soccer player was assistant coach for the Danish national soccer team and for Juventus Torino, where he was a key contributing factor to the Champions League title.

Bangsbo currently still works as a consultant for Juventus Torino.

Like Verheijen, Bangsbo advocates for a very soccer-specific approach to fitness training, although Bangsbo does use more drills off the ball than Verheijen.

More information and literature on Dr. Jens Bangsbo can be found on his website:

www.bangsbosport.com

5.8   SUMMARY OF PRESENTED PERIODIZATION MODELS

"Our goal is to help young players understand the game. Of course we value technique, which is where it all begins. But we want the players to learn how to think. We want them to learn how to run less, but smarter."

Pep Guardiola

All classic periodization models offer interesting approaches but do not offer a satisfactory all-in-one solution for soccer.

While the still widespread forms of classic periodization provide interesting basic knowledge, they are not sport specific and originate from track and field, swimming, and weight lifting, which is why they cannot possibly serve as the only basis for periodization in soccer.

The soccer-specific periodization methods also provide interesting input, but, nevertheless, these approaches do not capture the full complexity of soccer, while the Verheijen approach is the most likely to do so.

As mentioned in the beginning of the book, the goal in working with soccer players is to acquire excellent playing ability along with self-confidence, which can only be trained with a holistic approach that includes all performance-determining factors.

Die Formel hierfür lautet:

Tactics + technique + athleticism + mental factors

= playing ability = self-confidence

Itemizing the individual sub-items under these four factors would go beyond the scope of this diagram, which is why we will focus on one sub-item to exemplify the importance of a holistic soccer-specific approach.

The complexity of soccer becomes apparent when taking a closer look at the limiting playing level performance factor, **speed**, which most would categorize as a sub-item under athleticism, but that would only be half true.

According to Weineck, a soccer player's speed can be divided into seven different areas:
- Action speed
- Action speed with the ball
- Movement speed without the ball
- Reaction speed
- Decision-making speed
- Anticipation speed
- Cognitive speed

When taking a closer look at these seven areas that comprise soccer speed, it becomes obvious that the approach to these factors cannot be strictly athletic, like with a 100-meter runner.

Next to genetic factors, such as muscle fiber composition and athleticism, the complexity of soccer speed can only be trained properly by including mental factors as well as tactics and technique. These, with the exception of Verheijen's model, cannot be implemented in a soccer-specific way.

The **tactical periodization model** specifically takes into account this problem and, to date, is the only model that fully reproduces the complexity of soccer and presents a holistic approach, which we will now explain on the following pages.

The following quote from Mourinho provides a small preview of the **tactical periodization concept**:

"Who is the fastest man in the world? Let's assume it is Francis Obikwelu, who can run 100 meters in less than 10 seconds. He is very fast, and I don't know any footballer that could keep up with him in a 100-meter race. However, in a football match, 11 against 11, I think Obikwelu would be the slowest!"

Furthermore, Mourinho says:

"Here's another example: textbook case of a slow player is Deco. If we were to put him in a 100-meter race with other athletes he would make a fool of himself...he's probably loaded with slow-twitch muscle fiber instead of fast-twitch muscle fiber. However, on the pitch, he is one of the fastest players I know because pure speed has nothing to do with football speed. Speed in football is about analysis of the situation, reaction to stimulus, and the ability to identify it."

"Therefore, to me, working on individualized qualities or out of context from the complexity of the game is a serious mistake."

Summarized: Mourinho is absolutely convinced that the fastest sprinter in the world, Usain Bolt, would be the slowest player on the soccer field.

A cross-section of different periodization models

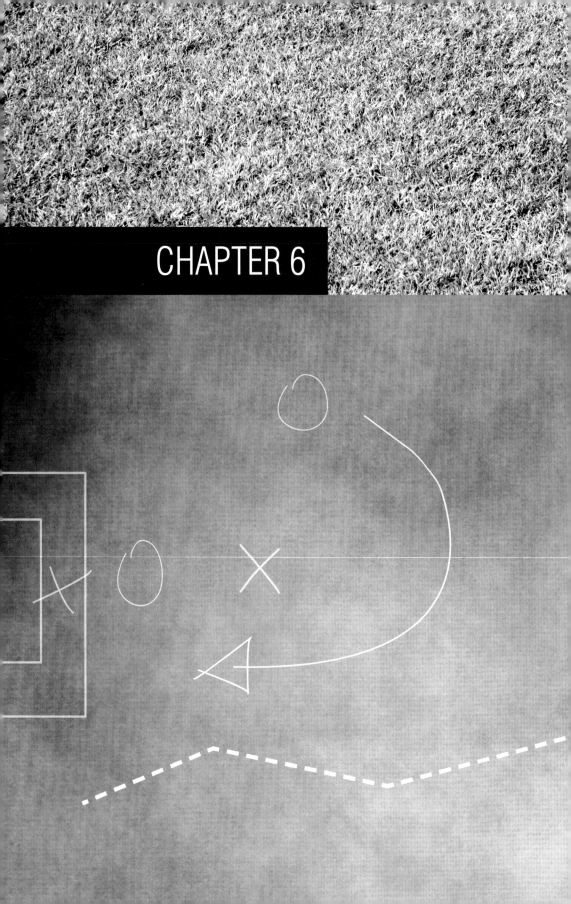

CHAPTER 6

Dualism, soccer mindset, and why performance should always be trained over competence

Dualism, soccer mindset, and why performance should always be trained over competence

*B*efore we introduce the tactical periodization concept, the following chapter will explain one more time why it is imperative that soccer training is soccer specific and holistic.

In the 17th century, the French philosopher, René Descartes, promoted the idea that mind and body are two different substances.

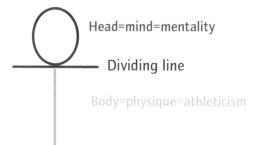

Head=mind=mentality

Dividing line

Body=physique=athleticism

Since then it has been scientifically proven that this notion of **dualism** is completely wrong.

The "mind" is in the brain and, thus, a part of the head, which, in turn, is a part of the body.

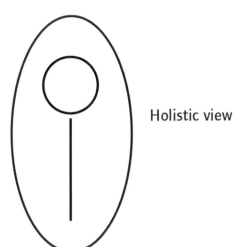

Holistic view

So why are there still soccer coaches who coach as though body and mind were two separate entities, as in the 17th century?

To bring more awareness to this very important topic, here is an example of something every soccer fan has likely experienced in some fashion.

Someone interested in soccer watches a soccer game and observes the behavior of team A, and, in doing so, describes the visible fitness level:

TEAM A	TEAM B	PLAYING TIME	FITNESS LEVEL
0	0	40 min	Fit!
0	0	50 min	Extremely fit!
0	1	60 min	Extremely fit?
0	2	70 min	Not fit!
1	2	80 min	Fit again?
2	2	90 min	Fit!
3	2	92 min	Extremely fit!

Surely you are familiar with this scenario...

As you can see, it is not possible to explain the process of players experiencing physical ups and downs by separating mind and body because how is it possible that the team is still **extremely fit** at 50 minutes, then **not fit** at 70 minutes after a goal deficit, and, suddenly, at 92 minutes, is once more **extremely fit**?

With a soccer-specific and holistic approach, it is no longer even necessary to talk about "mental" or "physical" because the body is seen as a unit and must also be trained as such in soccer.

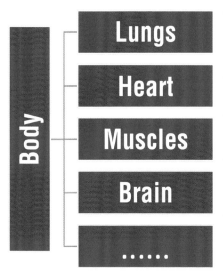

When taking a holistic view of a soccer player, we find an explanation:

After conceding a goal, negative thinking causes fewer hormones that are important to performance in soccer, like dopamine, adrenaline, or testosterone, to be released. This causes the player to appear visually less fit.

Thus, an important question in soccer is how to circumvent this problem.

The answer:

With a soccer mindset and POSITIVE PUSHING

What happened has happened and cannot be undone, like, for instance, in the above scenario, conceding a goal or making a bad pass or a bad call by the referee.

Instead of focusing on what happened and anything negative, players must develop a **soccer mindset** that allows them to focus just on the performance and block out anything they have no control over or any external factors. This can only be achieved from soccer-specific training where every drill entails consequences so that the players can develop this soccer mindset.

That is why soccer training should always focus on training performance rather than working separately on technique, athleticism, or mentality.

Every coach knows the "training champion" who possesses enormous **skills**, but who can't perform on the weekends, which is why training should not focus on skills but rather **performance**.

In soccer, in particular, it is extremely important to see the big picture while always keeping an inside-out perspective.

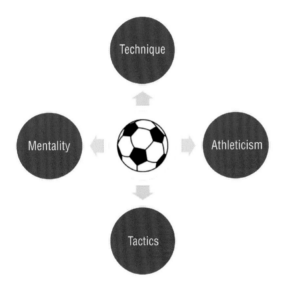

The soccer coach must ask himself how he can, for instance, adapt scientific trends in mentality to soccer.

Unfortunately, the opposite is often the case: a non-soccer athletic coach or a mental coach brings non-soccer models into soccer that are completely unrelated to the game and trains skills that are unrelated to soccer and have no bearing on performance.

When you travel to Germany and want to communicate, there are two options:

• All Germans must learn English.

• You learn German.

So why should all soccer players learn a new language instead of a stranger to soccer learning the soccer language so he is able to communicate his approaches?

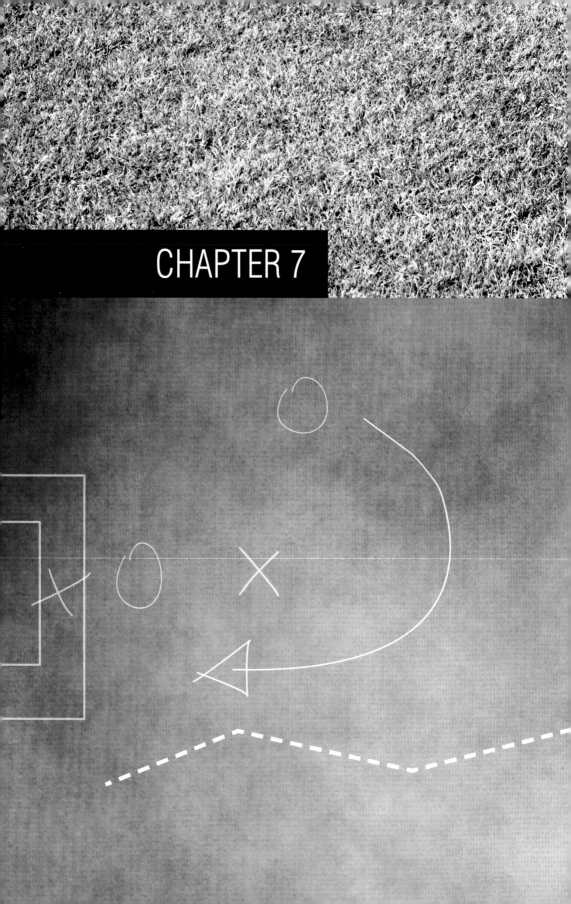

CHAPTER 7

The successful tactical
periodization concept—
A soccer-specific,
holistic, and tactical
approach

The successful tactical periodization concept—A soccer-specific, holistic, and tactical approach

Most prominent proponent of tactical periodization, "the special one"—José Mourinho, two-time Champions League winner

"We can differentiate between traditional analytical training where different contents are trained separately, integrated training that uses a ball but is still no different than the traditional method.

And then there is my training method, called tactical periodization. While many people think that tactical periodization has something to do with the two previously mentioned methods, it is a completely different approach."

*A*s the name suggests, **tactical periodization** is a soccer-specific periodization that prioritizes tactics.

In brief, the goal of tactical periodization is to conceptualize the implementation of a playing concept.

In doing so, a specific concept is created from a mix of tactical strategy as well as training and sport-scientific findings that is meant to reflect the basic tactical principles of a playing concept.

Originally, the "periodização táctica," or tactical periodization, is based on the ideas of Portuguese sport scientist, Vitor Frade, who developed this model in the 1990s and who is a mentor to José Mourinho and André Villas-Boas.

Also, the ideas and concepts of college professor, Fransico Seirullo of Spain, who coordinated athletic training at FC Barcelona, are and have been important contributions.

Vitor Frade—spiritual father of periodização táctica

Even if some coaching greats, like Ernst Happel, have pursued similar ideas in the past, the tactical periodization concept in its entirety is unique.

Previously, Louis van Gaal and Guus Hiddink also provided interesting and important input with their ideas, and Germany even had a coach, Volker Finke, who then worked for SC Freiburg and already structured his training based on this tactic and even back then used the implicit learning approach.

Cameroon's current national team coach, Volker Finke, was one of the first coaches in Germany to periodize his training based on tactical principles when he worked for SC Freiburg.

Surely the best known proponent of tactical periodization is José Mourinho since he is also the most successful proponent of this concept.

As previously mentioned, in tactical periodization, tactics always form the center of planning and training design because only with tactics can other performance factors, such as technique or athleticism, be transferred to a soccer game.

Tactics can be divided into three basic areas that build on each other:
- **Individual tactics**
- **Group tactics**
- **Team tactics**

As this list shows, team tactics initially always build on individual tactics.

Consequently, players must have excellent training in individual tactics and perfect 1-on-1-performance because this concept is based on perfect individual tactics.

It is logical that even the best team tactician cannot form a top team out of 11 players with weak individual tactics.

Most important about the tactical periodization model is the idea of a holistic approach that can show the complexity of the game.

The four performance factors in soccer are often trained independently of each other, and focus areas are set separately within the individual areas, which makes it impossible to project the complexity of the game:

Outdated and isolated approach to the four performance factors in soccer that only trains skills

Without this understanding of the complexity, individual components such as technique and speed cannot possibly be integrated into an overall game context.

Running fast is good...

But what good does it do in soccer if a player is always at the wrong place at the wrong time?

That is why in tactical periodization the four performance factors are never trained separately, and, as the name suggests, tactics are always at the center.

Holistic approach of tactical periodization: training performance

Any game situation a soccer player wants to successfully solve always requires the following factors to come together, beginning with a tactical decision:

- First, the player must make a decision (tactics).
- Next, he must execute a motor skill (technique).
- This, in turn, requires movement (athleticism).
- And it is always driven by emotions (mental factors).

The adaptation process that is triggered with complex and realistic soccer training is called **teleonomy**, which is the scientific term for targeted and purposeful behavior of organic systems that combines necessity and coincidence.

By the way, for all those who think that the tactical periodization model is only suitable for professional sports:

This model can easily be adapted to all ages and performance levels. For instance, the youth teams of the professional teams José Mourinho coaches are coached based on a holistic concept that builds on the skills that the professional team requires.

7.1   THE FOUR GAME PHASES AND TRANSITION PLAY

"Running is for animals. Soccer is about brains and the ball."

Louis van Gaal—current coach for Manchester United

A coach who wants to use tactical periodization must have mastery of the theoretical aspects of tactical periodization as well as understanding of the methodological principles. Consequently, the starting point for all considerations is a game model constructed by the coach.

At the outset, the most important question any coach should ask before developing a game model is:

How do I behave during the four phases of the game and especially during those game-deciding transitional moments?

The four, or rather five, game phases according to Louis van Gaal

This model provides players the answers to questions they must answer on the playing field:

* How do we behave when we have possession against team X and they are organized or unorganized?
* How do we behave when opponent X has possession and we are organized or unorganized?
* How do we behave when we transition from defense to offense against opponent X?
* How do we behave when we transition from offense to defense against opponent X?

When taking a closer look at teams that train according to the tactical periodization concept, it is obvious that most coaches place lots of importance on defense, followed by the transitional moments from which most goals originate.

The top teams that train with this concept are all characterized by very few conceded goals as well as perfectly organized defensive play with rehearsed pressing variations, showing they are able to adapt according to the game situation and opponent.

The poster coach for this model, José Mourinho, always gives his teams a perfect defensive structure first as a matter of principle.

The logic behind that is:

If you're keeping a clean sheet, it is impossible for the opponent to win.

This gives the players self-confidence and courage for the offense which is more difficult to train.

By building on this framework, the players are coached in minute detail on how to behave during the five phases.

"Great teams dominate space and ball. That means you dictate the game when you have the ball and you control the space when you defend."

Legendary coach, Arrigo Sacchi

7.2 IMPORTANCE AND DEVELOPMENT OF A GAME MODEL IN THE CONTEXT OF TATICAL PERIODIZATION

"A great pianist doesn't run around his piano or do push-ups on his fingers. He plays the piano."

The game is the best teacher.

When using tactical periodization, it is important to differentiate between a coach with a soccer ball and soccer coaching.

Most people think that simply doing all the drills with the ball is training according to the principles of tactical periodization.

The secret of tactical periodization is not the ball but rather the tactical goal of each of the drills used.

All drills are structured so they have a tactical focus that builds on a previously determined game model.

Many coaches want to practice different fitness-related factors in a realistic manner, so they, for example, enlarge the field during one form of play to emphasize endurance or make the field smaller to prompt actions that require explosive power.

This does not have much in common with the tactical periodization approach in which there is a firm belief that the focus must be on the tactic on which everything else builds.

This approach supposes that the training of physical factors should never be split up but that all factors must always be trained together—sport specific and based on the principles that develop from a game model.

In doing so, it is important to not run a lot, but rather to run the right way.

In order to provide the players the best possible training, it is vital to create an appropriate game model.

When a coach comes to a new team, he must first conduct an actual state analysis to then be able to develop a game model based on the resulting knowledge:

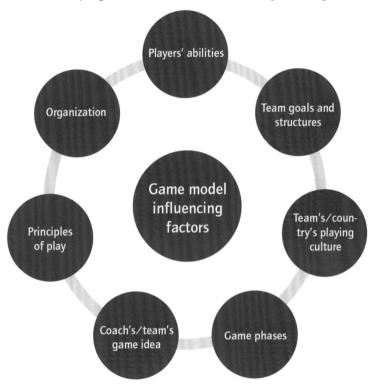

In this game model, the following questions must be answered:

- What abilities do the players have?
- What is the team's structure, and what are its goals?
- What characterizes the team's playing culture?
- Tactical behavior in the four game phases?
- What is the team's game idea?
- What are the principles of play?
- How is the team organized?

For instance, after his analysis at the beginning of his tenure as coach for Chelsea FC, José Mourinho commented that the present players did not fit his planned game model.

For Mourinho, this analysis is also important so he may know what atmosphere he needs to create to make his players comfortable.

In his opinion, players must be happy in all other areas of their lives to be able to achieve an optimal performance.

After this initial analysis, a game model is created that should reflect the coach's and the team's philosophy as well as the team's strengths and weaknesses.

"First is philosophy. The start of everything is you decide the style of play". – José Mourinho

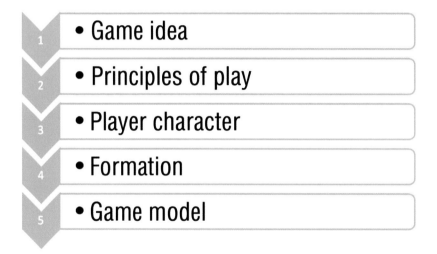

1. • Game idea
2. • Principles of play
3. • Player character
4. • Formation
5. • Game model

7.2.1 DEVELOPMENTAL STEPS OF A GAME MODEL IN DETAIL

"The best and only test for a soccer player is competing."

Sir Bobby Robson, head coach to the former assistant coach, José Mourinho, at FC Barcelona

Since no country, league, club, or team are the same, there can never be a universally valid game model, only an ideal game model for a team.

The game model is a team's DNA and makes each team unique.

The chosen game model should allow every player to maximize his potential within that model.

After his analysis, the coach must communicate his game model and his vision to the players, which is why it is important that the game model fits the team's character.

Ideally, the entire team then anticipates as one on game day because they have learned from the game model what to do in any given situation.

With a game model, the coach, thus, provides the players a structure with which the players then uniformly think and act on the field.

If the coach wants to entrench his game model, he must plan the concept as well as devise the concept's implementation.

Adequately communicating the intended game model is arguably the greatest challenge of the tactical periodization concept due to the number of different behaviors that must be taken into account.

First, a game idea or playing philosophy must be created that also takes into account the cultural conditions of a respective country.

The extremely well-structured Swiss Soccer Association, which received much praise after their U17 World Cup title in 2009, concisely characterizes its playing philosophy on its webpage as follows:

We play dynamic and open zone soccer:
- **Dynamics:** Our players run, fight, and give it their all to assert our game.
- **Offensive:** Our players attack and look for the finish at every opportunity.
- **Zone soccer:** Our teams are well organized, compact, and force the opponent to make mistakes.

To simplify communicating the game model after determining a game idea, establishing the principles for the five game phases, and customizing the basic orders and formations to the types of players, individual elements of the game are broken down into ever-smaller structures.

Here, the coach works up the desired behaviors under consideration of these points to subsequently break down the desired tactical behaviors in more and more detail:

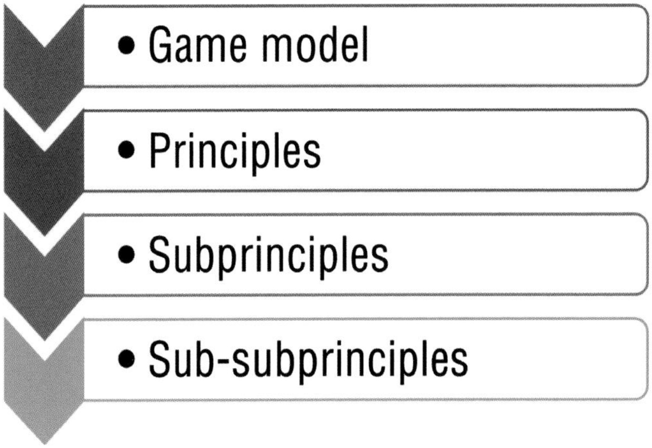

- **Game model**
- **Principles**
- **Subprinciples**
- **Sub-subprinciples**

1. **Game model as the top factor**
2. **Principles**
   - Game model substructure
   - Team tactics
3. **Subprinciples**
   - Substructure of principles
   - Group tactics
4. **Sub-subprinciples**
   - Substructure of subprinciples
   - Individual tactics

After these principles have been defined, basic formations and game systems that build on the existing players and characters and fit the game idea, principles, and players must be created.

If you would like more information on the subject of basic formations and game systems, my first book, *Successful German Soccer Tactics* (Meyer & Meyer Sport, 2015), might be the perfect choice.

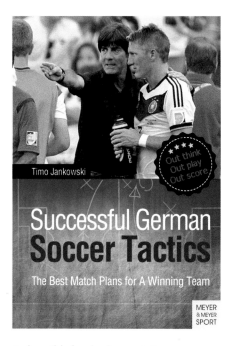

To buy this book please visit:

http://www.m-m-sports.com/successful-german-soccer-tactics-9781782550624. html

7.2.2 EXAMPLE OF THE TACTICAL BEHAVIOR PATTERNS BREAKDOWN

- **Game idea**

As per the Swiss Soccer Association

Zone soccer: Our teams are well organized, compact, and force the opponent to make mistakes.

Or:

A perfectly organized and compact defense takes the initiative to force the opponent to make mistakes.

- **Principle**
> Team tactics

How do I do that?

> Being dominant in phase 3: Opponent has possession/own team is organized.
> What would be the best way for us to behave?

For example, during a controlled midfield pressing, how must the team behave?

Precisely where do I want to capture the ball, or, how should the team be positioned during the opponent's goal kick?

- **Subprinciple**
> Group tactics: When the opponent has possession, how should the forwards behave, for instance, or the halfbacks, or the back four?

- **Sub-subprinciple**
> Individual tactics: How must the individual players behave in this phase?
> One example would be for the far forward to veer off toward the opponent's 6.

Summary:

The goal of a game model is to make complex situations simpler for the players by first disassembling the situation like a puzzle and then reassembling it step by step.

It is common knowledge that Mourinho uses a **color box system**.

For example, when Mourinho calls out "blue box" during a game, the team knows that they must intensely press the opponent.

If Mourinho calls out "green box," he wants his players to keep the ball within their ranks so they can rest.

Furthermore, while implementing his game model, Mourinho, as previously indicated, makes sure that the youth team game model is appropriately adapted to the pro team.

The game model must be seen as flexible and, thus, can be continuously refined, which is subject to an ongoing process.

1. Situation analysis: Diagnosis and prognosis
2. Organization of the training process: program planning
3. Program implementation: training
4. Evaluation and monitoring: product analysis

After the end of a game, the established game model can also be used as an evaluation tool for the game and the upcoming training week:

• How well did the team execute the game model on the field?

• Based on the game model and the upcoming opponent, how does the new training week need to be structured?

Once the game model is completely finalized, the entire season is as good as planned because all of the playing ability factors play a role within the game model. Therefore, they are practiced throughout the entire year.

Now the game model can be implemented during training, whereby the 8 methodological principles and the 10 biggest mistakes one can make with this concept play an important role.

7.3 THE EIGHT METHODOLOGICAL PRINCIPLES AND THE TEN BIGGEST MISTAKES ONE CAN MAKE WITH THE TACTICAL PERIODIZATION CONCEPT

"A good coach is one who helps his players maximize or discover their potential. That is his principal function."

Marcelo Bielsa—brilliant coach, currently coach at Olympic Marseille, previously Olympic champion with Argentina, national coach for Chile, and coach at Atlético Bilbao

The tactical periodization concept includes eight methodological (i. e., scientific method) principles that must be taken into account during planning and implementation.

7.3.1 THE EIGHT METHODOLOGICAL PRINCIPLES

"If you were quarter-inch out of position he would stop practice and put you in the correct position."

Thierry Henry on training under Pep Guardiola at FC Barcelona

1. Specificity principle

The goal of every training unit must be to improve the players' performance.

That is why all drills must relate to the game, which makes the specificity principle "the boss."

The purpose of this principle is to make each training exercise specific to the sport, the situations found in that sport, and the training goals.

That is why very abstract or very simple exercises are frowned upon, because they are not specific enough.

So every practice is a simulation of situations taken from the game model.

2. Operationalization principle

Extremely important is the operationalization of the game model and the tactical principles.

What is my game idea?

How do I behave in the five game phases?

Which drills can I use to practice the desired behavior?

The better the operationalization, the higher the degree of specificity.

3. **Hierarchical structure principle**

This principle is used to subdivide the tactical principles that originate from the game model to then break down tactical exercises into basic principles on which the exercises can then be built step by step:

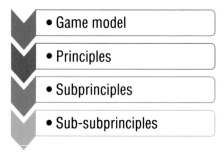

- Game model
- Principles
- Subprinciples
- Sub-subprinciples

The better the hierarchical division is structured, the easier it is for the players to implement the principles.

4. Horizontal variation of specificity principle

This refers to the specific control of intensity and the type of exercises used in the training process.

In horizontal variation, training should be structured in a way that allows the body to always optimally recover.

In doing so, the microcycle is periodized in a wave-like manner with the goal of fine-tuning the components so the players are optimally recovered physically and mentally for their next competition.

5. Performance stabilization principle

Achieving stabile performances is particularly important in professional sports.

FC Barcelona's fitness expert, Francisco Seirullo, stated that one of FC Barcelona's goals is for players to range between 70 to 80% of their optimal performance level without major fluctuations and to then elevate it to between 80 to 90% during the decisive championship phases in March and May.

To accomplish this, the conceptual composition of the microcycle is structured the same, week after week, in tactical periodization.

Another important point is the intensity, which, with the exception of the first day of the microcycle, is higher than the volume.

6. Conditioned exercise principle

It is important that movements that occur more frequently in a game are also practiced with corresponding frequency.

A central defender requires different movement sequences than a winger.

Imagine the 198-pound Jérôme Boateng training with the same endurance runs as the featherweight Philipp Lahm. The likely result: Boateng would be overworked.

But if Lahm did the same weight training as Boateng, Lahm would be completely overwhelmed.

That is why tactical periodization advocates using the same movements that players also execute in a game.

Since all exercises are based on the desired tactics, players are deployed in all exercises according to their own individual qualifications.

While there are no obvious structures in street soccer,

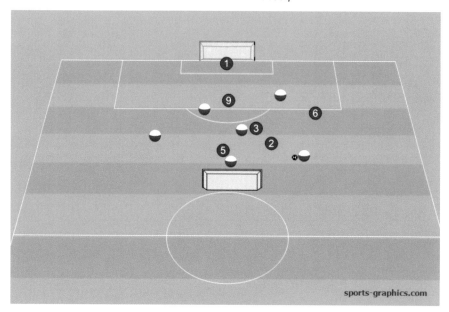

in tactical periodization, the implementation of every exercise is specific to position.

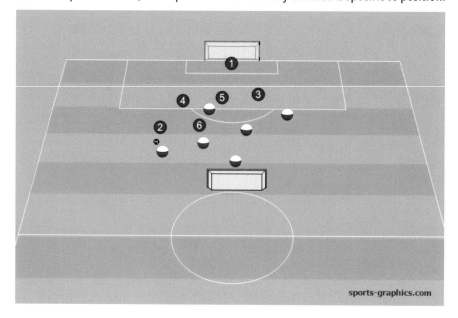

7. Complex progression principle

The complex progression principle can also be seen as the reduction principle of the game model's complexity.

Here, the planned progress is recorded—of course, primarily in regard to the principles derived from the game model.

In doing so, the hierarchical structure of the game model is primarily scrutinized to make sure that the players understand the different principles in order to make optimal learning progress.

8. Principle of tactical fatigue and concentration

The ability to concentrate plays an important role in achieving the best possible performance.

When the head is tired, it becomes difficult to concentrate, which has a negative effect on performance.

Tactical periodization assumes that head and body are closely linked.

On training days or during exercises that are tactically very demanding, the degree of tactical fatigue must be controlled.

7.3.2   TEN MISTAKES THAT SHOULD BE AVOIDED AT ALL COST

"It is not about training a lot. It is about training intensely."

Francisco Seirullo (in conversation with Pep Guardiola) is responsible for FC Barcelona's training concept. In 2006, he won the Champions League not only with FC Barcelona's soccer players, but also their team handball players.

	10 SOURCES OF ERROR WHEN USING TACTICAL PERIODIZATION
1	The description of the game model is not detailed enough.
2	Planning is vague.
3	Coaching is too nonspecific.
4	The game model is in incorrect sequence.
5	Too little demand is placed on players.
6	Time is wasted with excessive preparation of concepts that are not tactical in nature.
7	A leader lacks knowledge, losing credibility.
8	There is a monotonous training structure.
9	Drills instead of principles of play are practiced.
10	There is a lack of monitoring and improvement of training process..

7.4 MENTAL INFLUENCING FACTORS, TATICAL CONCENTRATION, AND THE IMPORTANCE OF SPECIFICITY AND REALISTIC INTENSITY

"As a soccer player I have made the most of my limited capabilities. And do you know why? Because I have passion. How could I have played more than 100 games for Argentina at my playing level! As a player I was mediocre. Everything I have accomplished I owe to my passion."

Diego Simeone, who also relies on the tactical periodization concept, was a world-class player and is a world-class coach (106 international appearances for Argentina as a player; Spanish national champion, and cup winner with Atlético Madrid).

At the highest level, many players often are on par technically, tactically, and athletically, which is why the following quote is so significant:

"Mindset beats quality".

Whenever José Mourinho takes over a new team, he shares his formula for success:

We are a TEAM.
Motivation + Ambition + Team + Spirit = Success

This formula confirms the importance of a good mindset.

Since everything originates from tactical considerations, training the mind is very important to the concept.

Here, the players' ability to concentrate is critical because due to soccer's high degree of complexity, players must be able to concentrate continuously for 90 minutes.

It is, therefore, important that the coaches ask their players to train at actual game speed.

The intensity needed to train realistically results from that concentration:

Intensity = Tactical concentration

Only with realistic intensity do the players reach the point where realistic tactical concentration takes place in their heads.

Thus, intensity is the basis of concentration, and every coach should strive to bring a high degree of intensity to his training.

According to Dr. Vitor Frade, it is essential that this intensity always be deployed in real time, which can only be ensured through realistic exercises.

Technical skills also play an important role here since a well-trained technique helps increase the players' attentiveness and improves their concentration.

"The ideal training session is that which reproduces the intensity and the emotions of competition."

Têle Santana—national coach for Brazil at the 1982 and 1986 World Cups

7.5   TEACHING LEARNING CONTENT IN TACTICAL PERIODIZATION

"Every coach knows about football. The difference is made in other areas."

José Mourinho with his leading players, John Terry and Frank Lampard

According to the mentors, the learning content of the tactical periodization concept should be taught using the *implicit learning approach and differentiated instruction.*

7.5.1   THE DIFFERENTIATED LEARNING METHOD

Every sport is characterized by specific movement sequences.

These movements can be taught through technical training, which builds an important foundation for subsequent performance.

There are two different learning methods for improving technique:

* "Grinding in"
* The differentiated learning method

While every technique in the soccer ABCs should initially be learned by *grinding in*—an ideal movement—the *differentiated learning method* should be used as soon as possible.

In soccer, a good practical approach is linking traditional training methods with the differentiated learning approach.

Differentiated learning is a new kinesiological learning approach in which basic movements are practiced in different ways.

So it is not about merely grinding in a movement, but it is also about variety of movement.

Suddenly, mistakes are viewed in a different light.

Mistakes traditional training methods want to avoid are deliberately built into the differentiated learning approach.

Scientists justify the differentiated learning approach with the argument that the identical repetition of an executed movement, such as an angled free kick, is most likely not possible, and one way or another, every soccer player has movements that are distinctly individual.

Another example would be the pass with the outside of the foot which many coaches curse.

But what if a player is good at this pass and is more comfortable with it than passing with the inside of the foot?

Differentiated learning is based on two important points:

1. All movements are subject to fluctuations and, therefore, cannot be repeated.
2. All movements are largely individual.

Contrary to traditional approaches, differentiated learning, therefore, has replaced the term, *mistake*, with the term, *fluctuation*.

In differentiated learning, fluctuations in the movement execution are considered necessary to advance the learning process and are used deliberately.

Ideally, when training a technique, there is variation in every single movement.

This forces the individual to constantly adapt to new situations, which is particularly important in soccer.

The major advantage is an intensified reaction of the central nervous system, which is highly activated due to the constantly changing sequences.

An example of differentiated learning in soccer using the shot on goal

The shot on goal could be trained with the following variations based on the differentiated learning approach:

- One eye closed (eye patch).
- Arm circles.
- One arm raised.
- Supporting leg in front or behind the ball.
- The ball is rolled up, passed, and dribbled before the shot.
- Different shooting techniques (instep, inside foot, toe kick).
- Vary the run-up (skip, kickbacks, high-knee skips).
- Shoot after juggling.
- In addition to the shot on goal, the player tosses a tennis ball in the air and catches it.
- Use different balls.
- There are no limits to creativity in differentiated learning.

Beyond that, fluctuations can be produced with forms of play, particularly, since the pressure of an opponent ensures that the ideal technique can virtually never be adopted completely from theory into practice.

Studies compared the effectiveness of differentiated learning to that of traditional approaches.

In soccer, major performance increases were achieved with the differentiated learning approach:

- Well-suited for large training groups, such as is the case in soccer.
- Lots of variety keeps soccer players motivated.
- More effective than traditional methods.
- In a game setting, players are able to react quickly to new and unfamiliar situations.
- More creativity in play.

7.5.2 IMPLICIT LEARNING

Horst Wein's training model already addressed this topic, but we would like to elaborate on the implicit learning approach here as it plays an important role in the tactical periodization concept.

In soccer, explicit—and also analytical—methods are prevalent so the players can acquire new learning content.

In doing so, a demonstration or verbal description of the learning objective is given first and is heavily coached.

Basic patterns are learned through exercise sequences that build on each other and increase in difficulty.

The ultimate objective is gradually achieved through practice and application in games.

But this method is not adequate for conveying a game model to the players because soccer is too complex to provide an analytical explanation for each individual situation.

This is why, during training, players are exposed to many different game situations in which they must independently identify problems.

The coach should do as little analytical coaching as possible, but rather get the players to familiarize themselves with the situation using the training form structure.

Thus, the coach can, for instance, tell his team that they must take a shot within a certain amount of time, which will shift the focus to quickly moving the ball forward and fast transitions from defense to offense.

Another option would be to make the number of touches the focus of the exercise, which can generate the pressure of increasing complexity.

As we already know from Raymond Verheijen, changing the size of the playing field and the number of players can also control the intensity of the game.

Combining the different control parameters can generate an extreme amount of complexity-related pressure. This trains the players' ability to concentrate, which is important in tactical periodization.

Achieving the desired objectives with this method requires the coach to have superior tactical understanding.

The purpose of every change is that the players implicitly learn the desired training goal without the coach having to explicitly point it out.

This motivates the players to think and learn and make decisions on their own.

"The secret to success in soccer can always be found in the training." Leo Beenhakker, legendary coach and winner of three consecutive championships with Real Madrid

7.6 MICROCYCLE—DETAILED WEEKLY STRUCTURING OF TACTICAL PERIODIZATION

"Players at this level don't accept what they're told simply because of the authority of the person saying it. We have to show them that we're right." – José Mourinho

Once the basic ideas of tactical periodization have been introduced and the structure of a game model and the most important facts and requirements have been addressed in detail, the next step is to introduce the basis of an optimal microcycle from this concept.

The structure of the training week plays a very important role in the design of the complete training process because the coach analyses the situation after each game and can specify important items for the upcoming opponent on the weekend.

The basic structure of the microcycle in tactical periodization must be absolutely consistent because, based on the principle of performance stabilization, this will lead to a consistent performance by the players.

Moreover, Mourinho's players already know five days before the next game who will start, which allows the players time to mentally prepare.

With the individual training units and concepts of the weekly plan, the players know exactly what they have to do and how they must play against the respective opponent.

7.6.1 WEEKLY SCHEDULE IN DETAIL

"You need both quality and results. Results without quality are boring. Quality without results is meaningless." – Johan Cruyff: Spieler- und Trainerlegende

Assuming there is a game on Sunday, the individual training days focus on the following items:

| | | | Recovery | | Game preparation | | | Recovery | |
		Sunday	Monday	Tuesday	Wednesday	Thursday	Friday	Saturday	Sunday
Tactical dimensions	Game complexity	Game day	Passive recovery	Active recovery	Medium-sized game segments	Large game segments	Small game segments	Game preparation	Game day
	Organization level			Subprinciples	Subprinciples Sub-subprinciples	Principles Subprinciples	Subprinciples	Subprinciples	
	Organization				Group work	Collective work	Group work		
Physical dimensions	Sub-dynamics			Active recovery	Specific strength training	Specific endurance training	Specific speed training	Active recovery	
	Strength			–	+++	++	+	–/+	
	Endurance			–	–	+	–	–	
	Speed			–	+	–	++	–/+	
Mental dimensions	Stress			–	+	++	–	–/+	
Training structure	Interruptions			+	++	+	+	++	
	Duration			90'	90'	90'	90'	60'	
	Spatial density Number of players/field size			+	–	++	+	+	

Day 1 (Monday)

It is known that José Mourinho gives his players a day off after a game even though he knows that from a physiological standpoint this is probably not ideal.

But here, too, Mourinho thinks globally and knows that each game is extremely demanding for the players in every area, and a day off allows the players to decompress and reenergize.

On that day, proper nutrition and sufficient sleep are particularly crucial.

Day 2 (Tuesday)

Subprinciples that will prepare the players for the demands of the upcoming game day are trained on the second day.

For example, the weekend's game analysis revealed that, for various reasons, the game build-up in the last game was not ideal.

This would result in the creation of a realistic passing drill in which players are organized based on position because each position on the field requires a different type of intelligence—that of the goal player is different than that of a center forward, for example.

Here, it is important that the players always have ample time to recover since the players must recover optimally, which is why the intensity and speed are reduced and the volume is slightly increased.

Following the passing drills, practicing positional play in larger spaces against obvious superior number situations is a good choice because it already prepares the players for the upcoming opponent.

Except for the training of shots on goal, the duration of each training session is realistic and lasts 90 minutes—the same as a game.

Day 3 (Wednesday)

In pro soccer, experience shows that after three days players might be physically recovered, but are not back up to 100% mentally.

Subprinciples and sub-subprinciples are, therefore, trained on this day because they are not too mentally demanding on the players, and the subprinciples involve teaching training content in small groups in which the players perform more explosive power actions.

Here, equal number games with fewer players, such as 2-on-2 or 5-on-5, are used primarily, and, as always, those are tactically linked to the game model.

Day 4 (Thursday)

Training on the fourth day mostly includes larger field sizes and distances in drills and forms of play that are very close to the distances in an actual game.

In addition, the volume of a unit is increased but does not exceed the intensity.

Here, the emphasis is primarily on the major principles that are fully implemented with the entire team, because for the major principles it is important to have 11-on-11 situations.

Set pieces are often also included in this training unit.

Day 5 (Friday)

On the fifth day, the focus is on subprinciples and soccer-specific speed. Quick decision-making plays an important role here.

For this reason, situations with fewer opposing players than in an actual game, such as 10-on-0 during the warm-up, are created, which will then transition into a 10-on-4 or 9-on-7, for example.

Another option that is used to train quick decision-making would be 8-on-8 or 10-on-10 drills on smaller fields.

In addition, the most important details from set pieces are repeated.

Day 6 (Saturday)

On the day before the game, it is all about preparing for game day.

Anything that might interfere is eliminated.

The complexity of drills is reduced, spaces are enlarged, and recovery time is extended.

The idea here is that the closer the training week gets to game day, the more important the ability to concentrate is, which would be diminished by overly intense training. That is also why the duration of training units is considerably reduced from 90 to 60 minutes.

Emphasis is primarily on subprinciples and sub-subprinciples.

"No one ever became a master without sweating." – Epiket (ancient philosopher)

7.7 TACTICAL PERIODIZATION OF TRAINING CONTENT AND THE GREAT ADVANTAGES OF POSITIONAL PLAY

"The fastest player isn't the one who can run the fastest; it is a player who can solve the game's problems the quickest."

Cesar Luis Menotti (1978 World Cup champion with Argentina)

From the strategic direction to developing a game model and the design of a microcycle, it is now time to plan the individual units.

Based on the principle of specificity, each unit (except for shot-on-goal training) has a 90-minute duration.

Here, too, the game model is consulted when planning the training units.

Here is an example of how tactical content can be periodized:

Periodization of training contents	Mesocycles			
	Microcycle 1	Microcycle 2	Microcycle 3	Microcycle 4
OFFENSE				
Game build-up in the back third	X		X	X
Game build-up in the middle third		X		X
Finish in the final third			X	X
TRANSITION TO DEFENSE				
Counterpressing		X	X	
"Diving"	X			X
DEFENSE				
Zonal defense ball in center		X		
Zonal defense ball on the wing	X			
High pressing			X	X
Midfield pressing			X	X
TRANSITION TO OFFENSE				
Counterattack			X	X
SET PIECES				
Offense		X		X
Defense	X		X	
POSITIONAL TRAINING	X	X	X	X

Appropriate drills must be developed iIf the game model design intends to dominate the opponent using short passes with brief touches and well-timed shifting play and lightning-fast deep passes, as well as quick counter-pressing, such as FC Bayern Munich does under Pep Guardiola.

All variations of positional play, which Pep Guardiola uses in every practice, are well suited to this purpose

"Everything that happens in a game except for the finish can also be done with a Rondo. The competitive aspect, the fight for it, creating space, behavior during possession and turnover, how to play 'one touch' soccer, how to get out of the cover shadow, and how to win the ball back."

Huge supporter of Rondos: Johan Cruyff, soccer legend

As the name implies, positional play practices the player's positional behavior.

In these Rondos, the team keeps the ball within its own ranks in tight spaces against an outnumbered opponent, such as FC Barcelona often does, whereby, because of the own superior number close to the ball, short passes with brief touches are being practiced.

The most commonly used Rondo here is the 5-on-2 in which the players circulate the ball on a field that is 8 x 8 meters (26 x 26 feet).

Why 8 x 8 meters specifically? This 8 x 8 meters is no coincidence, but rather rests on the idea that this distance is ideal for quick ball circulation on the one hand and, on the other hand, that the 8-meter distances are also ideal in a defensive block.

The goal is also for the players to perceive the situations on the extremely shortened field even more quickly and thus reduce the customary 0.3 seconds reaction time of a top athlete by half to 0.15 seconds in order to always stay one step ahead of the opponent mentally and physically.

Bayern pro players in a Rondo

Next to brief ball contacts, this is also a great way to practice counter-pressing.

Depending on training emphasis, these positional games can be controlled by field size, number of players, or coaching points.

Along with high intensity and concentration, the following coaching points must always be taken into account when practicing Rondos.

Getting out of the opponent's cover shadow

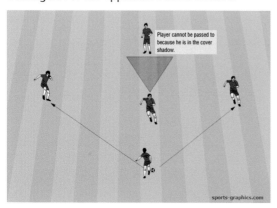

Getting open the right way is very important in Rondos. Players must be careful to avoid being in the opponent's cover shadow.

Creating good angles

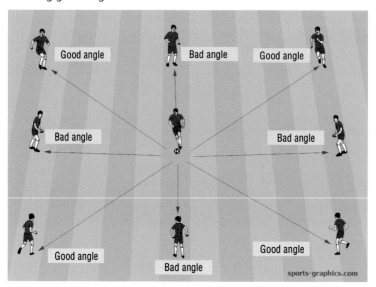

Whenever possible, players should position themselves at a 45-degree angle to the player in possession because this angle is ideal for continuing play. Of course, good passing on the angle is important.

Open body position and standby position

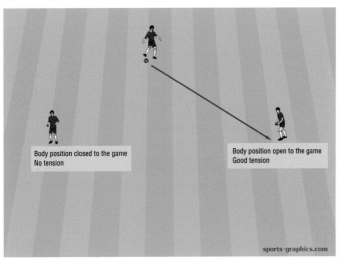

An open body position is extremely important so the player can be passed to, so he can observe as much of the situation as possible, and so he can be able to make the best decision for continued play.

Moreover, the players must be constantly at the ready and have good body tension.

Oriented ball control

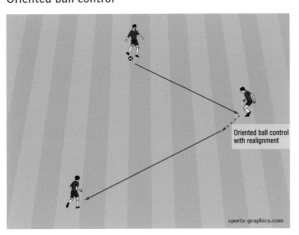

Oriented ball control is absolutely essential to keep ball speed high and to avoid the player pressuring himself as soon as he receives the ball. Rondos are the perfect way to practice this.

"A pass offers 36 different types of communication."

Forms of play in which possession play takes place in small spaces initially followed by scoring as quickly as possible after a number of touches specified by the coach or shifting play can be derived from these positional games.

Along with preventing injuries, the warm-up is already used for tactical work.

For instance, corresponding passing drills the coach has adapted to the game model and the opponent serve to optimally prepare the players for the continued progression of the training unit.

Based on the principle of conditioned exercise, the players are already classified by position during these initial passing exercises.

"The intention is not to move the ball, rather to move the opposition." – Pep Guardiola

Thus, according to Guardiola's game model, the first practice after a game day and a passive training day might look like this:

TRAINING OBJECTIVE: IMPROVING GAME BUILD-UP IN THE MIDDLE THIRD AND COUNTER-PRESSING					
Week: 26	DATE: June 22	DAY OF THE WEEK: Tuesday	DURATION: 90 minutes	WORKLOAD: Active recovery	TOTAL DURATION: 90 minutes
	WARM-UP	EXERCISE 1	EXERCISE 2	EXERCISE 3	EXERCISE 4
Type of exercise	Passing drill without counter-pressure Distance 12 meters	Positional play 4-on-1; 8 x 8 meters	Positional play 6-on-3; 20 x 20 meters	Positional play 10-on-6; 60 x 60 meters	8-on-8 plus goal player; 60 x 60 meters
SUBPRINCIPLES	Third-man running drill; Long balls	Oriented ball control; Recognizing open spaces	Creating superior numbers; Counter-pressing; Creating and narrowing spaces	Creating superior numbers; Counter-pressing; Creating and narrowing spaces	Defense: Collective shifting Offense: Implement exercises 1-3
SUB-SUBPRINCIPLES	Oriented ball control; Pass timing	Defensive behavior while outnumbered	Transitioning and recognizing open spaces;	Veering off Transitioning and recognizing open spaces	Play deep: Play through the lines Duels/individual tactics
DURATION	15 minutes	20 minutes	20 minutes	20 minutes	15 minutes

7.8   CONCLUSION AND THE SUPERIORITY OF TACTICAL PERIODIZATION

"Mourinho didn't teach me how to play football. I know how to play football. He taught me how to play in a team, which is something different. And that's why he is successful wherever he is."

Didier Drogba, Champions League winner and two-time African Soccer Player of the Year

The biggest difference between a coach who works with the ideas and concepts of tactical periodization and other coaches is that for his planning this coach can always build on his developed game model.

The training is completely realistic based on tactical principles that are specified in this game model, which gives the team a sense of security and allows it to continue to grow with each exercise.

An enormous advantage over other periodization methods used in soccer is that tactical periodization has a holistic approach, and soccer isn't divided into individual components. More importantly, every game situation is governed by a game model, which makes this approach more efficient than all the others.

Moreover, at the end of the day, only the facts matter, and these show that the tactical periodization model is currently the most promising concept, which is substantiated by the many titles won by the coaches who use this model, like José Mourinho or Pep Guardiola.

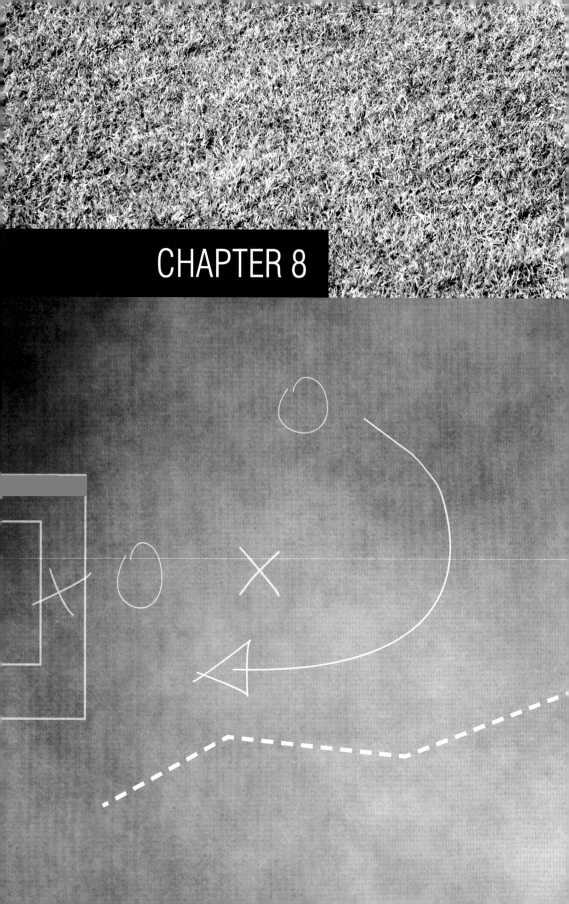

CHAPTER 8

More than 60 practical examples from top coaches and top youth academies

CHAPTER 8

More than 60 practical examples from top coaches and top youth academies

"Look at the best, learn from the best, be the best."

Pep Guardiola learned from Johan Cruyff

"You play as you train. Later, during the match, it depends on each individual player's talent whether the tactics are implemented or not. But the speed depends on the training. If your training is weak you will play weak. If you train obsessively you will play obsessively. And these guys train obsessively." – Pep Guardiola on soccer training

O n the following pages you will find more than 60 drills from the world's best coaches, professional teams, and youth academies that have been closely researched and reviewed.

All drills build on tactical considerations and training technique as well as mental factors and athletic components.

Breaking away behind a defender and third man running—Carlos Queiroz

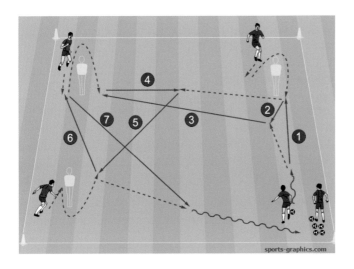

sports-graphics.com

Organization and progression

*   Set up three TOMs (training opponent mannequins) in a square 15 meters apart, as shown in the figure.

*   A dribbles up and plays a well-paced pass to B, who breaks away from behind the opponent with an intensive and lets the ball rebound.

*   Now the first player passes to the third player C at an angle, who has also broken away from behind the opponent and lets the ball bounce off to B, who will play the same sequence with the fourth player D, who then dribbles to the starting point after the final pass.

Duration

*   2 x 8 minutes (practice clockwise and counterclockwise)

Variations

- Number of contacts
- Change passing sequence
- Semi-active opponents

Coaching points

- **Tactics:** Breaking away from behind the opponent, third man running, timing
- **Technique:** Angled passes with both feet
- **Fitness:** Rhythm changes
- **Mindset:** Concentration, intensity, quality

"Living corners" Ronny Deila, Celtic Glasgow

Organization and progression

- Set up narrow twin penalty boxes with two goals (20-25 meters) and goal players.
- 4-on-4 plus two passers next to the goals.
- Objective: Playing deep to score as often as possible using the passers.

Duration

- 4-6 x 1.5-3 minutes

Variations

- Number of contacts
- Goals via the passers count double
- Position changes after a pass to an outside player

Coaching points

- **Tactics:** Running lanes, getting open, third man running, playing deep
- **Technique:** Passing, shot on goal, dribbling, feints, tackles, ball control
- **Fitness:** Realistic speed and endurance training
- **Mindset:** Duels, initiative, courage, self-confidence, joy **of playing**

Playing inferior/superior number 5-on-5—Chelsea London Academy

Organization and progression

- Laterally expand the penalty area to a length of 40 meters and mark the centerline.
- 5-on-5 on two goals with goal players.
- Three offensive players against two defensive players on each half, creating superior/inferior number play.
- Players must take a shot as quickly and as often as possible.

Duration

- 4-6 x 1.5-3 minutes

Variations

- Equal number play in the zones
- Player in possession is allowed to go into the next zone
- Limited touches

Coaching points

- **Tactics:** Getting-open behavior of offensive players; inferior number defense
- **Technique:** Passing, shot on goal, dribbling, feints
- **Fitness:** Realistic speed and endurance training
- **Mindset:** Winner mentality, self-initiative, courage, self-confidence

4-on-4 plus 1-on-1—Atalanta BC youth division

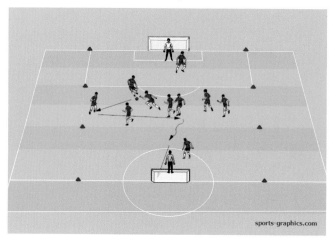

Organization and progression

- 48-meter field divided into three zones (three 16-meter zones).
- 5-on-5; one defender from each team stands in the respective defensive third.
- 4-on-4 in the middle zone.
- One offensive player from the middle zone must dribble into the attack zone, resulting in a 1-on-1.

Duration

- 3-5 x 2-4 minutes

Variations

- Limited touches
- No return passes
- Time limit for shot on goal

Coaching points

- **Tactics:** Getting-open behavior, transition behavior, group and individual tactics
- **Technique:** Passing, oriented ball control, dribbling, feints, tackles, shot on goal
- **Fitness:** Realistic speed and endurance training
- **Mindset:** Self-initiative, joy, **courage, perseverance**

Realistic endurance training from a triggered attack—Umberto Romano, assistant coach at FC Wohlen

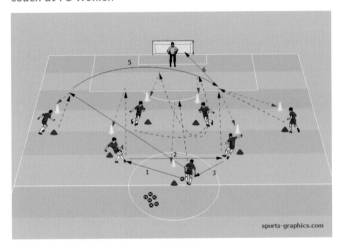

sports-graphics.com

Organization and progression

- Use cones to mark positions in the preferred basic offensive order.
- Position another cone 5-10 meters in front of each position.
- Perform an attack trigger that builds on the game principles and ends with a shot on goal. If no goal is scored, the players transition and return to the starting position at top speed.
- Next is an active recovery phase of 20-40 seconds (depending on the sprinting distance).

Duration

- Dauer: 4-6 min; 2-3 Serien.
- 3-4 min aktive Pause zwischen den Serien.

Variations

- Type of attack trigger
- Increase or decrease sprint distances
- 11 positions instead of seven as shown in the figure

Coaching points

- **Tactics:** Automating, act from the basic offensive order, running lanes, transition from offense to defense
- **Technique:** Dosing and timing of passing play, shot on goal
- **Fitness:** Intermittently realistic, rhythm changes, sprint readiness
- **Mindset:** Concentration, volition, quality, sprint readiness

Rondo 1: 4-on-2—Pep Guardiola

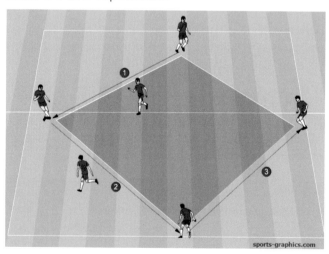

Organization and progression

- Six players play 4-on-2 for possession in a square measured at 10 x 10 meters.
- The players in possession play in diamond formation.
- The two remaining players who participate before the turnover go in the middle.

Variations

- Number of touches
- Mandatory touches
- Players in the middle link hands
- Change field dimensions

Duration

- 10-20 minutes

Coaching points

- **Tactics:** Play without ball, get out of cover shadow, open body position, quality of decision-making
- **Technique:** Oriented ball control, flat pass, timing and dosing
- **Fitness:** Realistic endurance training
- **Mindset:** Concentration, communication, intensity, "thinking for oneself"

Rondo 2: 5-on-3—Pep Guardiola

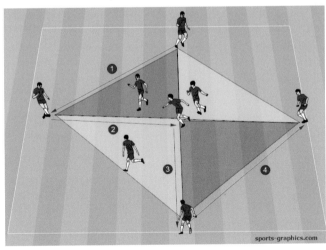

Organization and progression

- 5-on-3 for possession.
- Four players play in a diamond formation with a fifth player in the middle.
- The player who makes a mistake must go in the middle.

Variations

- Number of touches
- Mandatory touches
- Change field dimensions

Duration

- 10-20 minutes

Coaching points

- **Tactics:** Play without ball, get out of cover shadow, open body position, quality of decision-making, third man running
- **Technique:** Oriented ball control, flat pass, timing and dosing
- **Fitness:** Realistic endurance training
- **Mindset:** Concentration, communication intensity, "thinking for oneself"

Rondo 3: 8-on-2—Pep Guardiola

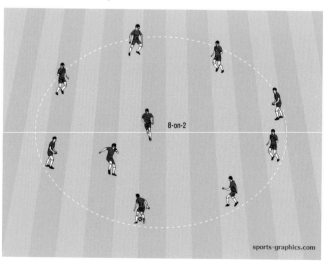

Organization and progression

- Eight players form a circle with a distance of 1 meter between players and engage in direct play for possession.
- Two players in the middle hunt for the ball.
- The last two players before a turnover must go in the middle.

Variations
- Players in the circle link hands
- Number of touches

Duration
- 10-20 minutes

Coaching points
- **Tactics:** Quality of decision-making, third man running
- **Technique:** Flat pass, passing frequency, timing and dosing
- **Fitness:** Realistic endurance training
- **Mindset:** Concentration, communication, fun, team spirit

Passing diamond—René Meulensteen/Manchester United

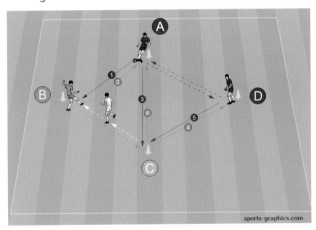

sports-graphics.com

Organization and progression
- Lay out a diamond using four markers, each 7 meters apart.
- Four players are positioned at the markers.
- A starts with a pass to B.
- Meanwhile, C pressures B.
- B plays the ball back to A and offers himself for a double pass.
- B plays the double pass to D, who passes back to B who is getting pressured by A and gets open for the double pass.
- B and C as well as A and D permanently change positions and tasks.

Variations

- Change the distance
- Build in touch variations
- 100% defensive action

Duration

- 2 x 7 minutes (1x clockwise, 1x counterclockwise)

Coaching points

- **Tactics:** Double pass, "no pressure, no ball", transition, change of position, change of pace
- **Technique:** Passing with both feet and proper pace at different angles
- **Fitness:** Realistic endurance training
- **Mindset:** Concentration and focus

Pass–sprint drill—La Masia, FC Barcelona

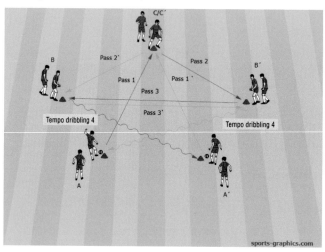

Organization and progression

- Position five markers 10-15 meters apart as shown in the figure.
- Two players at each position.
- A plays to C.
- C controls the ball and plays to B.
- B plays directly to B1.

- B1 does a tempo dribbling to A1.
  - When B1 has the ball, A1 brings a second ball into the game.
  - Each player sprints after his ball.

Variations

- Change the distance
- Vary touches

Duration

- 2 x 8 minutes/3 x 6 minutes

Coaching points

- **Tactics:** Play and support, change positions
- **Technique:** Passing with both feet and proper pace at different angles, dribbling
- **Fitness:** Realistic endurance training
- **Mindset:** Concentration, focus, sprint readiness

Passing drill Y1—Louis van Gaal

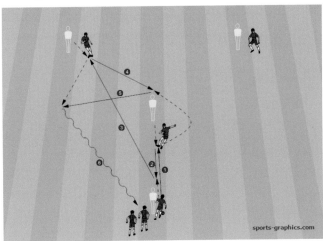

Organization and progression

- Set up four TOMs in a Y-shape 10-15 meters apart.
- A starts with a pass to B.
- B plays back to A.
- A plays through one line to C.

- B comes toward C to play a double pass.
- C dribbles back to the starting position.

Variations

- Change the distance
- Build in touch variations

Duration

- 2 x 8 min. (always 1 x clockwise, 1 x counterclockwise)

Coaching points

- **Tactics:** Play deep, outside sole of the foot turn, double pass
- **Technique:** Passing with both feet at a proper pace at different angles
- **Fitness:** Change of pace, realistic endurance training
- **Mindset:** Concentration, intensity, focus, communication

Passing drill Y2—Louis van Gaal

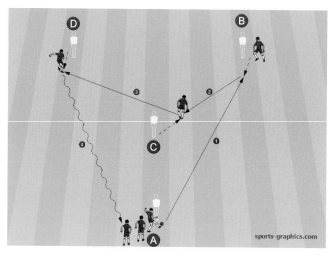

Organization and progression

- Set up four TOMs in a Y-shape 10-15 meters apart.
- With the first ball, A plays through a line to B, who comes toward him after making a contrary running motion (feint).

- B plays directly to C who plays at an angle to D.
- D dribbles back to the starting position.

Variations
- Change the distance
- Build in touch variations

Duration
- 2 x 8 minutes (always 1x clockwise, 1x counterclockwise)

Coaching points:
- **Tactics:** Play through lines, getting-open behavior
- **Technique:** Passing with both feet at a proper pace at different angles
- **Fitness:** Change of pace, realistic endurance training
- **Mindset:** Concentration and focus

Shot on goal after passing combination 1—Louis van Gaal

sports-graphics.com

Organization and progression
- Set up three markers in a diagonal line as shown in the figure.
- A starts from the base line with a pass to B.
- B lets the ball bounce back to A.

- A plays deep to C who starts toward the ball to play a double pass with B before the shot on goal.
- Each player moves to the next position.

Variations
- Change the distance
- Build in touch variations
- Semi-active opponents

Duration
- 2 x 7 minutes (1x clockwise, 1x counterclockwise)

Coaching points
- **Tactics:** Feint, look over the shoulder, double pass, deep play
- **Technique:** Passing with both feet at a proper pace, shot on goal
- **Fitness:** Realistic endurance training, change of pace
- **Mindset:** Concentration and focus, shooting instinct

Shot on goal after passing combination 2—Louis van Gaal

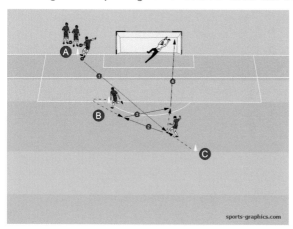

sports-graphics.com

Organization and progression
- Set up three markers in a diagonal line as shown in the figure.
- B asks for the ball, but then moves off in an arc.

- A plays deep in behind B toward the approaching C.
- C plays a double pass with B before the shot on goal.
- Each player moves to the next position.

Variations
- Change the distance
- Build in touch variations
- Semi-active opponents
- Specific type of kick for shot on goal
- Build in feints

Duration
- 2 x 7 minutes (1x clockwise, 1x counterclockwise)

Coaching points
- **Tactics:** Feint, look over the shoulder, play through lines, run an arc, double pass, deep play
- **Technique:** Passing with both feet at a proper pace, shot on goal
- **Fitness:** Realistic endurance training, change of pace
- **Mindset:** Concentration and focus, shooting instinct

Quick transition in different game phases—AC Milan

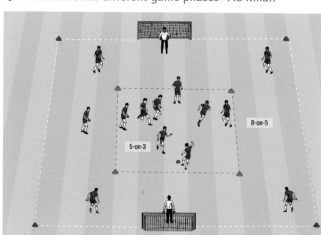

Organization and progression

- Mark a large square measured 40 x 40 meters. Mark a square 20 x 20 meters centered within the large square.
- Form two teams: team A has eight players, and team B has five players.
- This type of game begins with a 5-on-3 in the small square.
- When the two defenders win the ball, they pass to their teammates who are positioned in the large square.
- Now the five players from team B hunt for the ball. A plays for possession; when B wins the ball, they can try to score on both goals, which team A tries to prevent with quick transitions.

Variations

- Number of players
- Field size
- Number of touches

Duration

- 4-5 minutes

Coaching points

- **Tactics:** Quality of decision-making, transition behavior defense to offense and vice versa, hunt for the ball, positional play
- **Technique:** Oriented ball control, flat pass, timing and dosing
- **Fitness:** Speed, rhythm changes, sprint readiness while hunting
- **Mindset:** Concentration, communication, positive aggressiveness, "thinking for oneself"

Playing through lines and improving shifting movements—FC Red Bull Salzburg

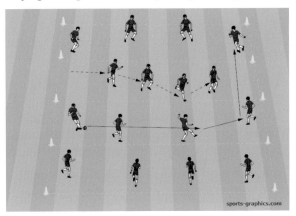

sports-graphics.com

Organization and progression

- Mark four rectangles that are 15-20 meters wide and 5-10 meters long.
- Form two teams of eight players each.
- Four players per field.
- The two teams try to play through the opposing back four.
- The team that plays defense can only act within its zone and tries to avoid balls into seams using skillful shifting.
- After winning the ball, change tasks.

Variations

- Form chains of three instead of chains of four.
- One opposing player is allowed into the opponents' defensive zone.
- Limit touches.

Duration

* 4 x 4 minutes

Coaching points

* **Tactics:** Back four shifting, recognize pass into seams
* **Technique:** Offensive—flat pass, dribbling approach; defensive—block
* **Fitness:** Aerobic and anaerobic endurance
* **Mindset:** Concentration and communication

Detailed image of the defensive team's shifting movements

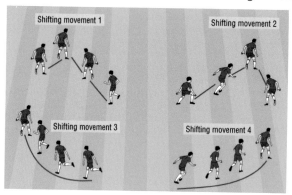

Position changes and getting open—Marcelo Bielsa

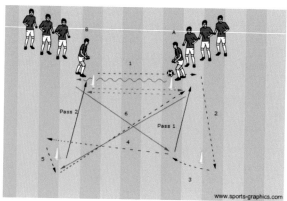

Organization and progression

* Set up four cones as shown in the figure.
* Set the first two cones 10 meters apart.

- Set the other two cones 15 meters apart.
- A, with the ball at his foot, and B switch positions at top speed.
- In addition, B sprints around the lower cone and receives the ball with his left foot and then plays to the starting cone of A, who sprints back.
- B keeps sprinting around the opposite cone and receives the ball with his right foot and plays to A at his starting cone.
- Next switch tasks.

Variations
- Number of touches
- Change distances
- Change passing order

Duration
- Each player completes 6-12 rounds in each of the two positions.

Coaching points
- **Tactics:** Play without ball, getting open, changing positions
- **Technique:** Flat pass, timing and dosing
- **Fitness:** Realistic speed training, change of pace
- **Mindset:** Concentration, communication, sprint readiness, quality

Soccer fitness in a 2-on-2—Dr. Raymond Verheijen

sports-graphics.com

Organization and progression

- 2-on-2 plus two goal players
- Set up a field that is 20 x 10 meters.

Duration

- 10 x 1.5 min.

Variations

- Number of touches
- Limit time for shot on goal
- No return passes to the goal player

Coaching points

- **Tactics:** 2-on-2 behavior
- **Technique:** Shot on goal, dribbling, feints, tackles, ball control, shielding the ball, passing
- **Fitness:** Realistic fitness training with lots of speed and strength actions, power
- **Mindset:** Winner mentality, decisiveness, duels, initiative, courage, self-confidence, joy of playing, concentration, intensity, perseverance

Realistic sprint-shot on goal under opposing pressure—Dr. Raymond Verheijen

sports-graphics.com

Organization and progression

- Mark off twin penalty areas with two goals and goal players.
- Lengthen the 16-meter line laterally.

- Two players always form a pair and on both sides start to the right of the goal post on the base line.
- The players look forward as the coach kicks the ball down the lane and react by chasing it at top speed and try to get a shot.

Duration

- Sprint endurance training: 10-second break until next sprint
- Speed training: 3 x 6 repetitions with 1-minute break between repetitions and 3-minute break between series

Coaching points

- **Tactics:** Anticipation
- **Technique:** Shot on goal
- **Fitness:** Sprint-repeating ability, speed
- **Mindset:** Concentration, perseverance

Ball into the seam—Peter Hyballa (Alemania Aachen, SK Sturm Graz) Bayer Leverkusen U19

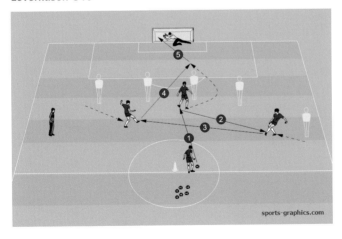

Organization and progression

- Set up four TOMs as a back four 20 meters from the goal; add two more markers as shown in the figure.
- The 6 plays to the approaching forward who passes at an angle to the outside midfielder.

- He plays a hard ball to the second forward who gets open and is moving toward him and plays the ball into the seam to his partner who finishes.

Variations

- Number of touches
- Create own passing sequence

Duration

- 20 minutes

Coaching points

- **Tactics:** Breaking away from the opponent, arced run, ball into the seam
- **Technique:** Shot on goal, flat pass, timing and dosing
- **Fitness:** Game rhythm change
- **Mindset:** Concentration, realistic intensity, communication, goal-scoring instinct

Offensive triangles—Pep Guardiola

1)

2)

3)

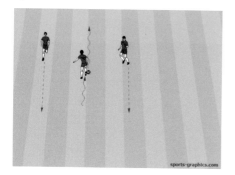

Organization and progression

- Three players form a triangle.
- One player is the Boss.
- Whenever the Boss plays a direct pass to his teammates, they let the ball bounce back off the far foot (figure 1).
- When the Boss stops the ball, the two switch positions (figure 2).
- When the Boss attacks the space, the other two must quickly form a new triangle on the other side (figure 3).

Variation

- Number of touches

Duration

- 3 x 3 minutes (switch Boss position)

Coaching points

- **Tactics:** Form triangles, correctly interpret movements
- **Technique:** Flat pass, timing and dosing
- **Fitness:** Realistic endurance training
- **Mindset:** Concentration, communication

Triangle formation defense—Pep Guardiola

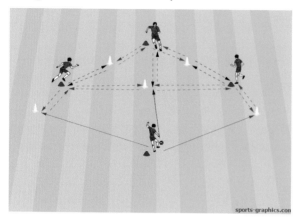

Organization and progression

- Position four cones 6 meters apart as shown in the figure.
- Place five additional yellow cones 3 meters from the red cones.
- Players start from the red cones.
- The Boss plays in front of one of the yellow cones, and the player in that space must start at that cone to play a direct return ball.
- If the Boss plays into the middle, the outside players safeguard with the triangle.
- If the Boss plays to the outside, the two far players move in to the next yellow cones.
- The moment the player has the ball back at his foot, these players must sprint back to their red starting cone.

Variations

- Number of touches
- Distances
- Increase number of players

Duration

- 4 x 1-2 minutes (switch Boss position)

Coaching points

- **Tactics:** Shifting movements, triangle formations, safeguarding
- **Technique:** Flat pass, timing and dosing

- **Fitness:** High intermittent training, power training
- **Mindset:** Concentration, communication, sprint readiness, volition training

Ball hunt: 5-on-2 with field change—Rudi Garcia/AS Roma

Organization and progression

- Mark two squares measured 12 x 12 meters.
- Two teams with five players each.
- The teams play 5-on-2 direct for possession in their square, 10 passes earning one point. If the two defenders win the ball, they pass to their teammates in their square, and two players from the other team then hunt for the ball.

Variations

- Raise degree of difficulty by making the triangle smaller
- Number of touches
- Three players hunt

Duration

- 4 x 4 minutes

Coaching points

- **Tactics:** Pressing, transition behavior, quality of decision-making, defense with inferior number
- **Technique:** Oriented ball control, flat pass, timing and dosing
- **Fitness:** Aerobic and anaerobic endurance, rhythm of play
- **Mindset:** Concentration, communication, "thinking for oneself," positive aggressiveness

Quick vertical play—Arsène Wenger

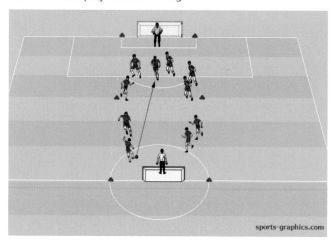

Organization and progression

- Mark a narrow lane that is 18 meters wide and 45 meters long.
- 5-on-5 plus goal players.
- Open play with offside.
- No return passes.

Variations

- Raise degree of difficulty by making the lane narrower
- Number of touches

Duration

- 4 x 4 minutes

Coaching points

- **Tactics:** Transition behavior in both directions, quality of decision-making, forward running paths
- **Technique:** Oriented ball control, flat pass, timing and dosing, shot on goal
- **Fitness:** Realistic speed, rhythm of play
- **Mindset:** Concentration, communication, positive aggressiveness, duels

10-on-10 and 1-on-1—Arsène Wenger

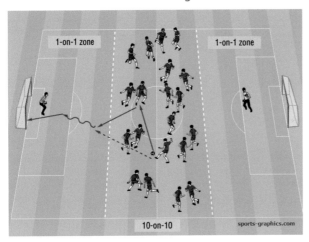

Organization and progression

- Entire playing field.
- Game starts with 11-on-11 in a designated zone between two defensive lines.
- When a player is able to get past the defensive line with a dribble or a forward pass, one of the defenders is allowed to come along into this defensive zone for a 1-on-1.

Duration

20 minutes

Variations

- Number of touches
- Open play, but both teams try to stay in the zone

Coaching points

- **Tactics:** Team tactics in offense and defense
- **Technique:** Passing, shot on goal, dribbling, feints, tackles, ball control, shielding the ball
- **Fitness:** Aerobic and anaerobic endurance
- **Mindset:** Winner mentality, decisiveness, duels, initiative, courage, self-confidence, joy of playing, concentration, communication, intensity

Position-specific speed training after triggering an attack—La Masia, FC Barcelona

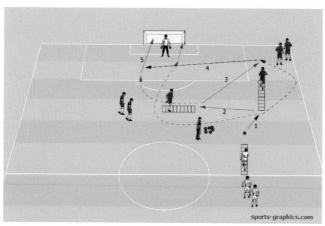

Organization and progression

- Set up three agility ladders as shown in the figure.
- The players simultaneously move through the ladders as many times as possible.
- White plays to red who plays at an angle to blue.
- Directly after his pass, white runs past and receives the forward pass from blue.
- Blue and red sprint into the box and overlap to utilize the ball from white.

Variations

- Adapt progression to own game model
- Instead of agility ladders, build in hurdles for jumps or slalom poles

Duration

- Each player completes six sprints at each station.

Coaching points

- **Tactics:** Getting-open behavior, offensive movement patterns like passing and overlapping
- **Technique:** Flat pass, crossing technique, shot on goal
- **Fitness:** Realistic speed training
- **Mindset:** Concentration, communication, goal-scoring instinct

Mirror moves—Wiel Coerver

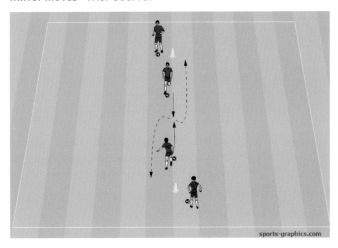

Organization and progression

- Set up two cones 12 meters apart.
- Both players do a fast dribble toward each other and execute the same feint.
- In doing so, they try to mirror each other.

Variation

- Change the feints (e.g., step-over, Zidane, Rivelinho)

Duration

- 4 x 4 minutes

Coaching points

- **Tactics:** Feel for distance, cognitive abilities
- **Technique:** Dribbling, feints, agility on the ball
- **Fitness:** Aerobic and anaerobic endurance, change of rhythm of play
- **Mindset:** Concentration, communication, intensity, field of vision

1-on-1 in different zones and distances—Wiel Coerver

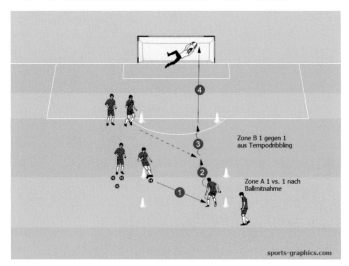

Organization and progression

- Use six cones to mark two zones.
- Zone A is 5 meters, and zone B is 10 meters.
- Player 1 makes a hard pass to player 2 and attacks.
- Player 2 tries to reach zone B with the first touch where he plays a 1-on-1 against player 3 to win and finish.
- Defenders can only defend in their respective zone.

Variations

- Change the distances
- Add a third zone

Duration

- 15-20 minutes

Coaching points

- **Tactics:** 1-on-1 offensive and defensive
- **Technique:** Oriented ball control, flat pass, dribbling, feints
- **Fitness:** Realistic speed, change of rhythm of play
- **Mindset:** Concentration, communication, positive aggressiveness, courage, perseverance

Feint + pass + transition—Ricardo Moniz (Tottenham Hotspurs, Hamburg SV, FC Red Bull Salzburg, Ferencváros TC, 1860 Munich)

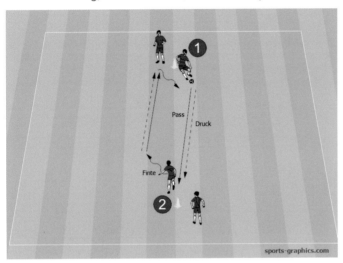

Organization and progression

- Set up two cones 12 meters apart.
- 1 plays to 2 and sprints after the ball to put realistic, but semi-active, pressure on 2.
- Player 2 does a feint and completes the same sequence after the feint.

Variations

- Change the distances
- Type of feint (e.g., step-over, Zidane, Rivellino)

Duration

- 4-6 x 2-4 minutes

Coaching points

- **Tactics:** Transition behavior
- **Technique:** Passing, ball control, feints
- **Fitness:** Aerobic and anaerobic endurance, change of playing rhythm
- **Mindset:** Concentration, communication, intensity

3-on-3 at six goals—Ajax Amsterdam Junior Academy

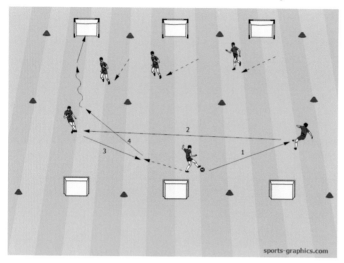

Organization and progression

- Set up six mini goals on a field measured 30 x 30 meters.
- Play is 3-on-3.
- Objective is to clear one side using quick ball circulation or to score a goal by winning 1-on-1 situations.

Variations

- Number of players
- Field size
- Eight goals
- Additional goals at sides

Duration

- 2 x 8 minutes

Coaching points

- **Tactics:** Shifting movements, creating superior numbers
- **Technique:** Passing play at different distances, dribbling, feinting
- **Fitness:** Realistic endurance and speed training
- **Mindset:** Concentration, communication, positive aggressiveness, intensity

Fast play forward in a 4-on-2—Swiss Soccer Federation

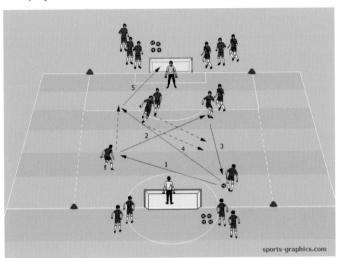

Organization and progression

- Laterally extend the penalty area to the centerline.
- Form two teams of eight players each and two goal players.
- The offensive team starts the action at the own goal with a diagonal forward ball.
- The next ball is a direct through ball to one of the two forwards, and a 4-on-2 is played to the finish.
- If the defenders win the ball, they can counterattack on the other goal while the offense tests the chances for a counter-pressing and quickly transitions to trying to win back the ball.
- Important: Play realistically with offside.

Variations

- A volley is played to the goal player after the ball is won.
- Instead of a 4-on-2, complete a 3-on-1 or 6-on-3.

Duration

- 20-25 minutes

Coaching points

- **Tactics:** Defend with inferior numbers, counterattack, play deep
- **Technique:** Technique and precision, dribbling, feints
- **Fitness:** Speed, realistic endurance, explosive power
- **Mindset:** Volition, courage, positive aggressiveness, goal-scoring instinct

4 x 1-on-1—Swiss Soccer Federation

Organization and progression

- Set up twin penalty areas with two goals and goal players at a 40-meter width.
- Designate two outside zones from the 5-meter area to the 16-meter area.
- Four players spread out in the two central and two outside zones so each field has one defensive and one offensive player.
- Open play, but players can only operate in their own zone.
- Objective is to create different 1-on-1 situations in different spaces.

Duration:

- 4-6 x 1.5-3 minutes

Variations

- Number of touches
- Limit amount of time for shot on goal
- 2-on-1 superior numbers during offensive action
- Passer

Coaching points

- **Tactics:** Offensive and defensive 1-on-1 situation
- **Technique:** Shot on goal, dribbling, feints, tackles, ball control, shielding the ball
- **Fitness:** Strength, explosiveness, change of rhythm
- **Mindset:** Winner mentality, decisiveness, duels, initiative, courage, self-confidence, joy of playing, power

Tactical shooting drill 1—José Mourinho

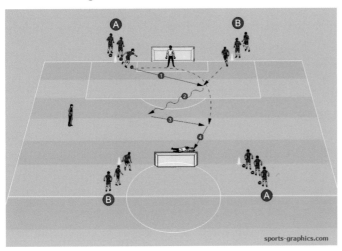

Organization and progression

- Set up two goals 40 meters apart.
- Players spread out next to posts.
- Two players try to get off a shot as quickly as possible with the following sequence:
    - A plays into the space to B and runs past.
    - B attacks the space with a fast dribble and plays into the space to A, who finishes.
- Afterward, switch tasks.

Variations

- Countdown finish within 6 seconds
- Number of touches

Duration

- 15-20 minutes

Coaching points

- **Tactics:** Counterattack, timing
- **Technique:** Oriented ball control, dribbling, pass into open space, shot on goal
- **Fitness:** Soccer-specific speed training
- **Mindset:** Concentration, communication, intensity, goal-scoring instinct

Tactical shooting drill 2—José Mourinho

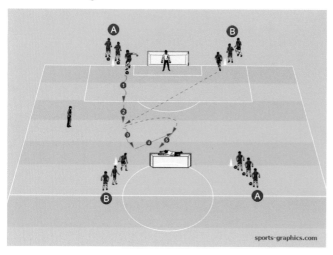

Organization and progression

- Set up two goals 40 meters apart.
- Players spread out next to posts.
- Two players try to get off a shot as quickly as possible with the following sequence:
  - A attacks the space with a tempo dribbling and passes to B who runs past.
  - B plays the ball to A who is sprinting toward the goal and then finishes.
- Afterward, switch tasks.

Variations

- Countdown finish within 6 seconds
- Number of touches

Duration

- 15-20 minutes

Coaching points

- **Tactics:** Counterattack, timing
- **Technique:** Oriented ball control, dribbling, pass into open space, shot on goal
- **Fitness:** Soccer-specific speed training
- **Mindset:** Concentration, communication, intensity, goal-scoring instinct

Tactical shooting drill 3—José Mourinho

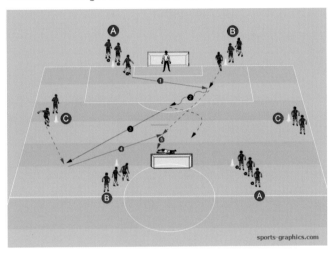

Organization and progression

- Set up two goals 40 meters apart.
- Players spread out next to posts.
- Position two outside players at two additional markers.
- Three players try to get off a shot as quickly as possible with the following sequence:
    - A plays into the space to B who controls the ball and plays a long ball to C.
    - B and A overlap and utilize C's cross.
- Afterward, switch tasks..

Variations

- Countdown finish within 6 seconds.
- Number of touches

Duration

- 15-20 minutes

Coaching points

- **Tactics:** Counterattack, timing, wing play
- **Technique:** Oriented ball control, dribbling, pass into open space, crossing technique, shot on goal
- **Fitness:** Soccer-specific speed training
- **Mindset:** Concentration, communication, intensity, goal-scoring instinct

4 x 3-on-1—José Mourinho

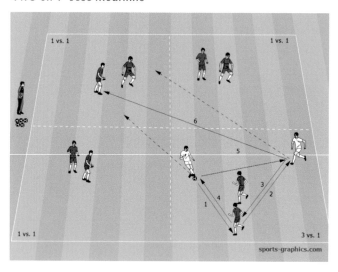

Organization and progression

- Mark four squares measured 10 x 10 meters.
- Form two teams of four players plus two neutral players.
- One player from each team is in a square.
- The two neutral players complete a 3-on-1 with the player in possession. Switch fields after five passes.

Variations

- Raise degree of difficulty: make the rectangle smaller
- Number of touches
- Specify number of touches at which field change must take place

Duration

- 4 x 4 minutes

Coaching points

- **Tactics:** Transition behavior, quality of decision-making, superior numbers play, quick perception
- **Technique:** Oriented ball control, flat pass, timing and dosing
- **Fitness:** Aerobic and anaerobic endurance, change of playing rhythm
- **Mindset:** Concentration, communication, positive aggressiveness, intensity

7-on-7 zone soccer—Dr. Jens Bangsbo

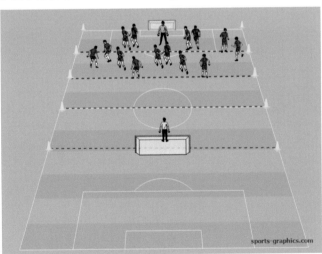

sports-graphics.com

Organization and progression

- Divide three-quarters of a playing field into four zones.
- 7-on-7 plus goal players.
- Open play.
- All players except for the goal players must always stay in two directly adjacent zones.

Variations

- Number of players
- Specify number of passes per zone after which players must leave the zone
- Each team must be in one zone
- Number of touches

Duration

- 4 x 4 mintes

Coaching points

- **Tactics:** Compactness, organization, transitioning
- **Technique:** Oriented ball control, flat pass, timing and dosing, dribbling, shot on goal
- **Fitness:** Aerobic and anaerobic endurance, change of playing rhythm
- **Mindset:** Concentration, communication, positive aggressiveness, intensity

2 x 1-on-1—PSV Eindhoven

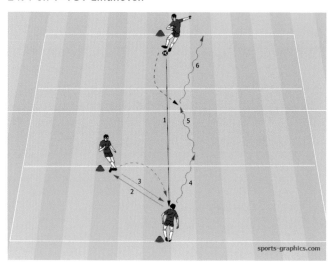

Organization and progression

- Set up three zones 10 meters apart.
- Player 1 plays a hard ball to player 2 who lets it bounce off to the side to player 3 and then has the ball directly returned to him.

- Player 3 plays a 1-on-1 in the first zone with the return pass to player 2.
- If player 2 makes it into the next zone, a 1-on-1 ensues against player 1, whereby he tries to dribble across the final line.
- After the pass, the outside players switch with the passer.

Variations

- Make the zones smaller or larger
- 2-on-1 in all zones

Duration

- 12-15 minutes

Coaching points

- **Tactics:** Individual tactics
- **Technique:** Oriented ball control, direct play, dribbling, feinting
- **Fitness:** Realistic speed training, change of pace
- **Mindset:** Concentration, communication, positive aggressiveness, courage, power, perseverance

Third-man running drill—Guus Hiddink

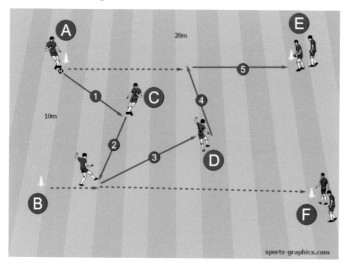

Organization and progression

- Set up a rectangle measured 10 x 20 meters, and select 8-10 players.
- A opens to C who plays sideways into the running path of B.
- B plays to D and sprints to the opposite cone.
- B plays into A's running path and immediately offers himself for the first pass from the other side.
- A plays a long ball to E, where the sequence starts from the other side.
- C and D stay where they are.

Variation

- Drill with two balls simultaneously from both sides

Duration

- 15 minutes

Coaching points

- **Tactics:** Open position to the game, third man running
- **Technique:** Flat pass at different angles, timing and dosing
- **Fitness:** Change of pace
- **Mindset:** Concentration, communication, intensity

Passing in an infinite loop–Hansi Flick (German Football Association)

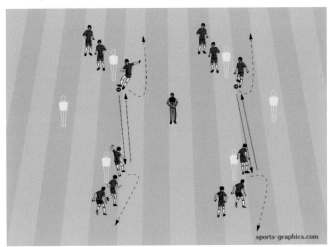

Organization and progression

- Set up TOMs 15 meters apart as shown in the figure.
- Form two groups.
- Evenly arrange the players behind the opposing TOMs.
- The players briskly start toward the ball and play it hard to the other side and then break away to the rear with an explosive movement.
- In doing so, the players always keep their eyes on the ball.

Variations

- Number of touches
- Specify manner of ball control

Duration

- 10 minutes

Coaching points

- **Tactics:** Automating—start toward the ball and immediately break away
- **Technique:** Oriented ball control, flat pass, timing and dosing
- **Fitness:** Aerobic and anaerobic endurance, change of playing rhythm
- **Mindset:** Concentration, communication, intensity

Breaking away from the opponent plus oriented ball control—Hansi Flick
(German Football Association)

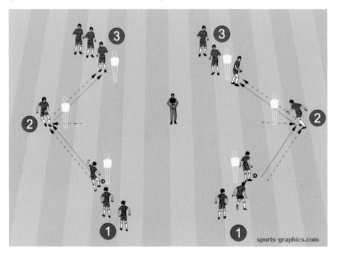

Organization and progression

* Set up six TOMs as shown in the figure.
* Position one player at each of the middle TOMs.
* 1 plays a hard ball to 2, who has broken away with an explosive movement and controls the ball and passes it to the other side.
* Player 1 runs to position 2 and completes the same movement to the other side.

Variations

* Number of touches
* Build in a double pass

Duration

* 10 minutes

Coaching points

* **Tactics:** Break away from opponent
* **Technique:** Oriented ball control, flat pass, timing and dosing
* **Fitness:** Aerobic and anaerobic endurance, change of playing rhythm, explosive break-away
* **Mindset:** Concentration, communication, intensity

Play in diamond formation with a volley—Inter Milan Juniors

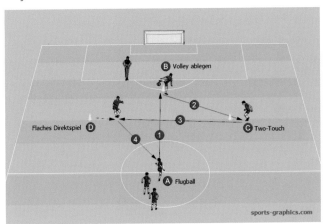

Organization and progression

- Mark a diamond with four cones set 30-40 meters apart.
- A opens with a volley to B.
- B must pass the volley to C from the air.
- C meets the ball and controls the ball into the space and plays a hard pass to D...
- ...who briskly moves toward the ball and passes directly to the starting position.
- The players follow the played ball.

Variations

- Vary the touches at the respective cones
- Change distances

Duration

- 15 minutes

Coaching points

- **Tactics:** Diamond play
- **Technique:** Volley, pass the volley, oriented ball control, flat pass, timing and dosing
- **Fitness:** Aerobic and anaerobic endurance, change of playing rhythm
- **Mindset:** Concentration, communication, intensity, quality

Trigger play between the lines and ball into the seam—Marcelo Bielsa

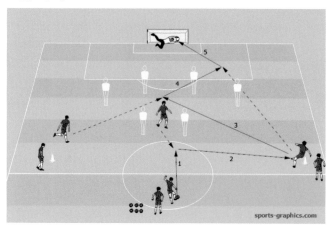

Organization and progression

- Use TOMs to set up a back four and two 6 players.
- One 6 opens long to 10.
- 10 plays an angled ball to the right outside player who plays a long ball to the left midfielder who is sprinting to the middle.
- Right after his pass, the right outside player moves in behind the back four where he receives the left midfielder's ball into the seam.

Duration

- 20-25 minutes

Variations

- Number of touches
- Limit time for shot on goal
- Adapt sequence to own game model

Coaching points

- **Tactics:** Tactical behavior during triggers in offense, ball into seam
- **Technique:** Passing game, timing of final ball, shot on goal
- **Fitness:** Change of pace, realistic sprint training
- **Mindset:** Concentration, communication, intensity, goal-scoring instinct

Fast play forward–Roger Schmidt/Bayer 04 Leverkusen

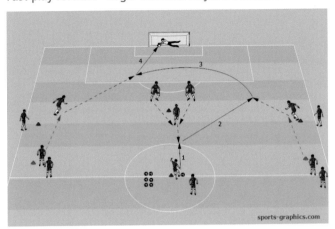

Organization and progression

- Assign four cones to the red offensive players and position the blue players as shown in the figure.
- Place two blue cones 10 meters away from the red cones at the outside positions.
- The drill opens with a long ball to the forward who is sprinting toward it. He lets the ball bounce back, and the first player has the choice of playing a long pass to the two outside players to the left or right.
- A soon as player 2 lets the ball bounce back, the defensive players on the outside positions spring into action.
- A counterattack with equal numbers ensues, but with a favorable starting situation for the offense.

Variations

- Shorten distances
- Limit time for shot on goal

Duration

- 20-25 minutes

Coaching points

- **Tactics:** Counterattack, transitioning
- **Technique:** Passing, shot on goal, crossing technique
- **Fitness:** Realistic speed training
- **Mindset:** Concentration, communication, intensity, quality, power

Counterattack 1: transition to offense—Jürgen Klopp/BVB

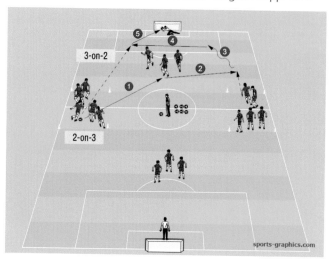

Organization and progression

- Mark two rectangles measured 10 x 10 meters as shown in the figure.
- Form two 3-on-2 teams in each rectangle.
- Add two central defenders and one forward per team on both sides.
- Two players play inferior numbers for possession.
- When the superior numbers team wins the ball, it tries as quickly as possible to play to the approaching forward and finish the counterattack in a 4-on-4.

Variations

- Limit time for shot on goal
- Equal numbers in the yellow rectangle

Duration

- 20-25 minutes

Coaching points

- **Tactics:** Counterattack
- **Technique:** Passing game, shot on goal, dribbling, feints, tackling, ball control
- **Fitness:** Strength, explosiveness, change of playing rhythm, soccer sprints at different distances
- **Mindset:** Winner mentality, decisiveness, duels, initiative, courage, self-confidence, joy of playing, concentration, communication, intensity, power

Counterattack 2: transition to offense—Jürgen Klopp/BVB

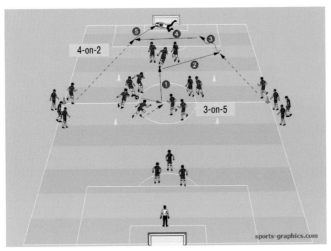

Organization and progression

- Mark a rectangle measured 20 x 20 meters as shown in the figure.
- Three players play against five to hold on to the ball in the rectangle.
- Position two additional central defenders and one forward per team on both sides as well as offensive players for both sides.
- When the superior numbers team in the yellow rectangle wins the ball, it plays a long ball as quickly as possible to the forward who tries to find the net in 4-on-2 with the two outside players.

Variations

- Limit time for shot on goal
- Equal numbers in yellow rectangle
- After the forward ball, all players move forward after the ball

Duration

*   20-25 minutes

Coaching points

*   **Tactics:** Counterattack
*   **Technique:** Passing game, shot on goal, dribbling, feints, tackling, ball control
*   **Fitness:** Strength, explosiveness, change of playing rhythm, soccer sprints at different distances
*   **Mindset:** Winner mentality, decisiveness, duels, initiative, courage, self-confidence, joy of playing, concentration, communication, intensity, power

Counterattack 3: transition to offense—Jürgen Klopp/BVB

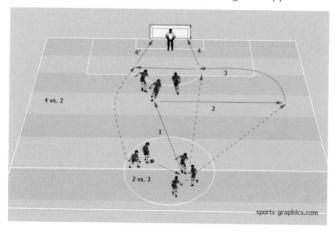

Organization and progression

*   Two players play for possession against three players in the center circle.
*   When the superior numbers team wins the ball they play a long ball to the forward to then get a shot on goal in a 4-on-2.

Variations

*   Limit time for shot on goal
*   Equal number circle
*   After winning the ball, all players move forward

Duration

- 20-25 minutes

Coaching points

- **Tactics:** Counterattack
- **Technique:** Passing, shot on goal, dribbling, feints, tackling, ball control
- **Fitness:** Strength, explosiveness, change of playing rhythm, soccer sprints at different distances
- **Mindset:** Winner mentality, decisiveness, duels, initiative, courage, self-confidence, joy of playing, concentration, communication, intensity, power

Circulating the ball in a back four—Christian Gourcuff

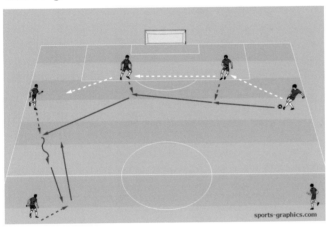

sports-graphics.com

Organization and progression

- Realistic positioning of a back four and the two outside midfielders.
- The players quickly try to move to the side to get the midfielder into the game.
- If this is accomplished, he quickly goes back to the other side.
- It is important for players to move with the ball.

Variations

- Number of touches
- Build in volleys
- Add a 6
- Build up to 10-on-0

Duration

• 20 minutes

Coaching points

• **Tactics:** Build-up in back four, "moving up"

• **Technique:** Offensive position techniques, ball control, quality passes

• **Fitness:** Aerobic and anaerobic endurance

• **Mindset:** Concentration, communication, intensity, quality

6-on-3 possession play and quick transitioning at four goals—FC Sochaux Juniors

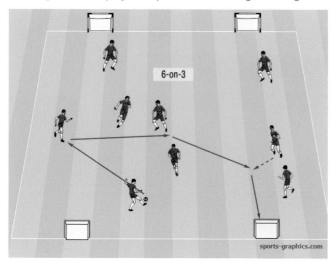

Organization and progression

• Four goals in a square that is 30 x 30 meters.

• Six players try to keep the ball in their ranks against three players.

• When the inferior numbers team wins the ball, they try as quickly as possible to get a shot at one of the four goals.

Variations

• Number of touches

• Limit time for shot on goal

• Number of players/field size

Duration

4 x 4 minutes (inferior numbers players switch after each round)

Coaching point

- **Tactics:** Quick ball circulation, transition behavior in both directions
- **Technique:** Passing, dribbling, ball control techniques
- **Fitness:** Aerobic and anaerobic endurance, change of playing rhythm
- **Mindset:** Initiative, concentration, communication, intensity

Recognizing open spaces: 8-on-8 with four corners—Manchester United

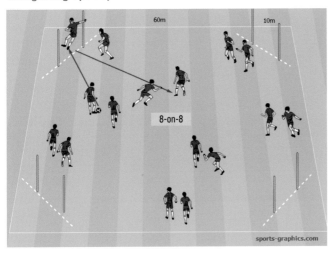

Organization and progression

- 8-on-8 on a field that is 60 x 60 meters.
- Set up four corner goals as shown in the figure.
- A goal is scored when the ball is played through one of the corner goals and then passed to a third player by a teammate.

Variations

- Number of touches
- Point scored when dribbling through a goal

Duration

- 3 x 8 minutes

Coaching point

- **Tactics:** Reading the game, getting-open behavior, shifting play
- **Technique:** Passing at all distances and in all forms, ball control, holding on to the ball
- **Fitness:** Realistic endurance training
- **Mindset:** Duels, initiative, concentration, communication, intensity

Blocking technique in a duel—Marcelo Bielsa

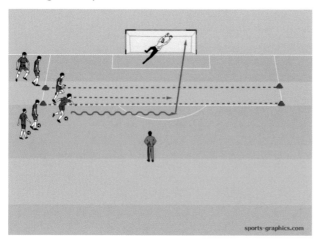

Organization and progression

- Set up a 2-meter wide corridor along the inside of the 16-meter line for the defensive players.
- The offensive player decides when to start with the ball at his foot and tries to get a shot without entering the zone.
- The defensive player tries to block the ball.

Variations

- Limit time for shot on goal
- Offensive player can enter the zone after a certain number of touches

Duration

- 3 x 6 repetitions with maximum power

Coaching point

- **Tactics:** Individual offensive and defensive tactics
- **Technique:** Blocking techniques, dribbling, feints, tackling techniques, shot on goal
- **Fitness:** Strength, explosiveness, change of playing rhythm
- **Mindset:** Winner mentality, decisiveness, duels, initiative, courage, self-confidence, concentration, intensity, power, perseverance

10-on-0—Lucien Favre/Borussia Mönchengladbach/Benno Möhlmann/FSV Frankfurt

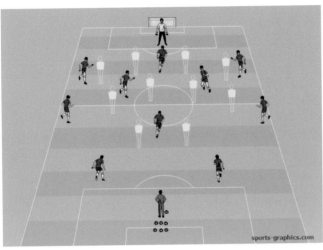

Organization and progression

- Set up 10 TOMs correspondent to the opponent's basic order.
- The coach opens the game.
- The players try to bring attacks that correspond to the game model to a successful finish at a realistic pace.

Variations

- Number of touches
- Limit time for shot on goal
- Build in semi-active or active opposing players
- Transition after finish

Duration

- 20-25 minutes

Coaching points

- **Tactics:** Initiate play, team tactical offensive behavior
- **Technique:** Shot on goal, dribbling, feints, ball control
- **Fitness:** Change of pace, aerobic and anaerobic endurance
- **Mindset:** Concentration, communication, intensity, initiative, determination

5-on-2 positional play plus obstacles—FK Austria Wein

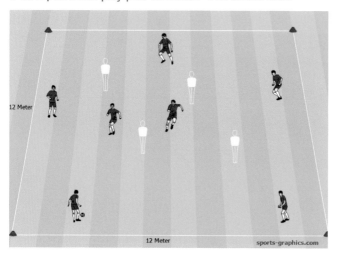

Organization and progression

- Set up a square that is 12 x 12 meters.
- Set up TOMs inside the square.
- 5-on-2 for possession.

Variations

- Number of touches
- Change TOM's
- Position a central passing station

Duration

- 10-15 minutes

Coaching points

- **Tactics:** Positional play, possession play
- **Technique:** Techniques for oriented receiving and controlling of the ball, passing techniques, direct play
- **Fitness:** Aerobic and anaerobic endurance
- **Mindset:** Concentration, communication, intensity

Bobinho positional play—Brazil

sports-graphics.com

Organization and progression

- 3-on-1 with one defender who must stay within a triangle that 5 x 5 x 5 meters.
- The three players in possession can score a point by making a successful pass to another player through the triangle.

Duration

- 10-15 minutes

Variations

- Number of touches
- Change size of triangle
- Limit amount of time in which a pass must be played through the triangle

Coaching points

- **Tactics:** Positional play, recognizing when to play through the lines
- **Technique:** Techniques for oriented receiving and controlling of the ball, passing techniques
- **Fitness:** Aerobic and anaerobic endurance
- **Mindset:** Concentration, communication, patience

8-on-8 on 3 goals—David Moyes/Rayo Vallecano

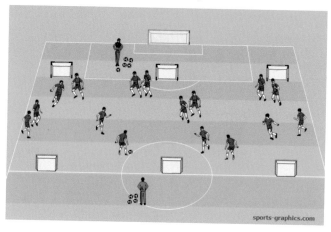

Organization and progression

- 8-on-8 on three goals
- Open play

Variations

- 6-on-6, 7-on-7, 9-on-9
- Change field size
- Number of touches

Duration

- 3 x 8 minutes

Coaching points

- **Tactics:** Play without ball, transition behavior, quality of decision-making, playing deep, quick ball circulation, shifting play

- **Technique:** Ball control with open body position, flat pass, timing and dosing
- **Fitness:** Aerobic and anaerobic endurance, changing of playing rhythm
- **Mindset:** Concentration, communication, positive aggressiveness, intensity, joy of playing, determination

Quick combination and shot in a 10-on-10—FC Valencia

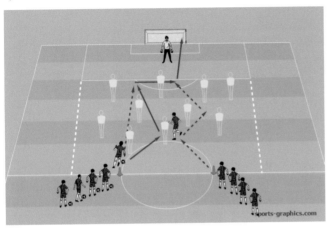

Organization and progression
- Set up TOMs in a corridor between extended 16-meter line and centerline.
- Two players try to get a shot on goal as fast as possible by quickly circulating the ball around the TOMs.

Variations
- Raise degree of difficulty: more TOMs or smaller field
- Limit time for shot on goal

Duration
- 15 minutes

Coaching points
- **Tactics:** Quick combination play, getting-open behavior
- **Technique:** Oriented ball control, flat pass, timing and dosing, dribbling, crosses, shot on goal
- **Fitness:** Realistic speed training
- **Mindset:** Concentration, communication, intensity, determination, power

Quick combination play with five players and shot on goal–ZdenÐk Zeman/AS Rome/SSC Naples

Organization and progression

* Categorize five players by position.
* After a pass from the coach, the players start with the ball at the centerline.
* The objective is to get a shot on goal at a realistic pace using combinations that are in line with the principles of play.

Variations

* Semi-active/active opposing players
* Limit time for shot on goal

Duration

* 15 minutes

Coaching points

* **Tactics:** Quick combination play, getting-open behavior
* **Technique:** Oriented ball control, flat pass, timing and dosing, dribbling, crosses, shot on goal
* **Fitness:** Realistic speed training
* **Mindset:** Concentration, communication, intensity, determination, power

Realistic speed training in a duel—Martina Voss-Tecklenburg/Swiss women's national team coach

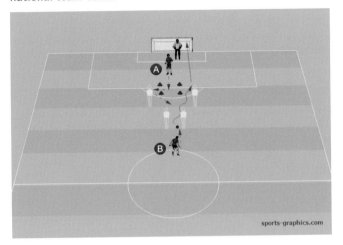

Organization and progression

- Use cones to set up two small goals .5 meter apart on the 16-meter line and two TOMs for goals 3 meters wide on the sides.
- Player A starts through the first goal 7 meters from the first cone goal and immediately afterward through one of the two subsequent cone goals on the sides.
- At the same time, B starts for the ball from the same distance as A, runs up to the open cone goal on the side, and then dribbles through one of the two goals in a 1-on-1.
- A defends the two goals on the sides.
- If B's dribbling is successful, he can take a shot on goal.

Variation

- Change distances

Duration

- 15 minutes

Coaching points

- **Tactics:** Individual tactics, perception
- **Technique:** Dribbling, changing direction, shot on goal

- **Fitness:** Realistic speed training, power
- **Mindset:** Competition, perseverance, concentration, communication, intensity, determination

Transition and counter-pressing drill—Martina Voss-Tecklenburg/Swiss women's national team coach

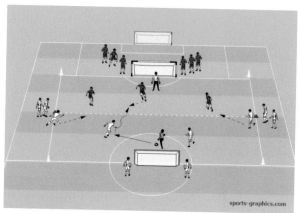

Organization and progression

- Set up two goals with goal players. The field length should be penalty area to centerline, and the field width should be 2 meters wider than the penalty box.
- Use two teams with 16-20 players.
- Two players from team A start with a pass from the goal player for a 2-on-3 against B.
- If team B wins the ball with skilled double-teaming, they transition and immediately try to score a goal.
- At the same time, two additional players from team A come onto the field for a 4-on-3 counter-pressing and try to win the ball and score.

Variations

- Limit time for shot on goal
- Limit touches

Duration

- 20 minutes

Coaching points

- **Tactics:** Quick combination play, getting-open behavior
- **Technique:** Oriented ball control, flat pass, timing and dosing, dribbling, shot on goal
- **Fitness:** Realistic speed training
- **Mindset:** Competition, concentration, communication, intensity, determination, perseverance

Soccer fitness in a passing circle—Hervé Renard, African champion with Zambia and Ivory Coast

sports-graphics.com

Organization and progression

- Set up two diamonds with 10-meter distances within the diamond and 17-meter (average sprint distance in soccer) from one diamond to the other.
- Use 4-6 players per diamond.
- The players play direct passes to each other within the diamond.
- At the coach's signal, the group leaves the ball behind and sprints to the other diamond, where direct passes resume immediately.

Variations

- Specify number of touches
- Players follow their passes within the diamond

- Juggling the ball instead of passing
- Change distances

Duration

- 4 x 4 minutes, two-minute active break after each series

Coaching points

- **Tactics:** Play in diamond formation, transition
- **Technique:** Passing
- **Fitness:** Realistic, intermittent endurance training
- **Mindset:** Volition training, concentration, quality

Moving forward from the midfield—Mauricio Pochettino/Tottenham Hotspurs

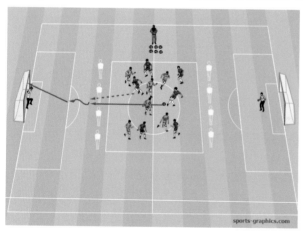

sports-graphics.com

Organization and progression

- Field size depends on number of players; use a minimum of six players plus two goal players.
- Mark a ball possession box in the center with four TOMs at each end of the box toward the goal.
- After 10 played balls, the team in possession is allowed to play a long forward ball that is challenged by a sprinting midfielder.
- 1-on-1 against the goal player.

Variations

- Limited number of touches
- One defensive player is allowed to chase the long ball.
- Two offensive players against one defensive player outside the box.

Duration

- 20 minutes

Coaching points

- **Tactics:** Group tactics, deep play, forward running lanes of midfielders, counter-pressing
- **Technique:** Technique under extreme pressure of time and from the opponent, final ball, shot on goal
- **Fitness:** Realistic endurance and speed training
- **Mindset:** Concentration, communication, intensity, the will to finish

1-on-1 with opposing pressure from behind—Tim Lees/Wigan Athletic and FC Liverpool Juniors

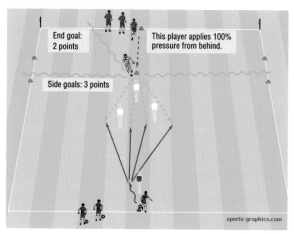

Organization and progression

- Approximately 75% of all ball handling at the top of the field takes place under pressure from the opponent, which this exercise is perfectly suited for.
- Mark two squares measured 20 x 20 meters with one end line and two side goals (3 meters).
- Red uses a feint to get around the opposing player and must determine in which space the green player is moving in order to outplay him at the correct pace.
- As soon as red has passed the ball, green gets 100% pressure from behind by a blue player.
- Green has two choices: either dribble through one of the side goals after settling the ball, which would give him one point, or across the end line, which would give him two points.
- Players switch by rotation.
- Realistic movements are important in this drill.

Variations

- Change distances
- Blue can apply pressure as soon as green moves.
- Red adds additional pressure from the front.

Duration

- 15 minutes

Coaching points

- **Tactics:** Offense: 1-on-1 with pressure from opponent from behind; defense: 1-on-1; anticipate the first ball
- **Technique:** Oriented ball control and tempo dribbling
- **Fitness:** Realistic speed training
- **Mindset:** Perseverance, concentration, intensity, resilience

Drill to improve pressing and to resist pressing—Johnny McKinstry, national team coach for Sierra Leone

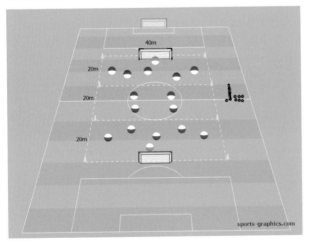

Organization and progression

- Use a playing field that is 60 meters long and 40 meters wide.
- Divide field into three 20-meter-long zones.
- Two teams of seven players plus goal players with offside.
- 2-on-2 in the middle zone.
- Three defenders against two attackers in the two goal zones.
- Players stay in their zones and play with two touches.
- A point is scored when a flat pass can be played to the goal player, which can also be done from another zone.

Variations

- Limited touches
- The player in possession can go into the adjacent zone.
- Goals can be scored in both directions.

Duration

- 20 minutes

Coaching points

- **Tactics:** Pressing, active pressure on the player in possession, defend forward, quick combination play, getting-open behavior
- **Technique:** Technique under extreme pressure of time and from opponent
- **Fitness:** Realistic speed training
- **Mindset:** Concentration, communication, intensity, resilience, positive attitude towards defensive work, patience during possession

More than 60 practical examples

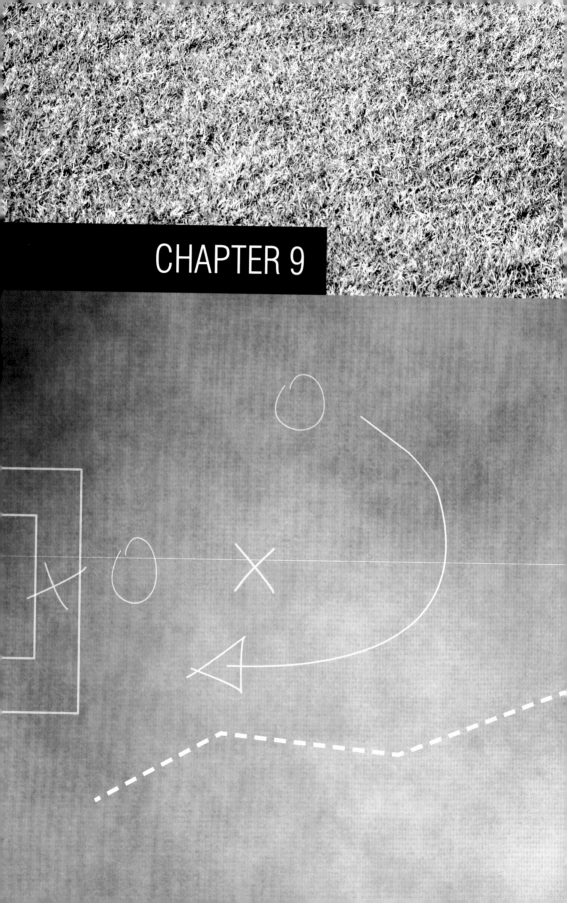

CHAPTER 9

Last but not least—
Contentment vs. gratitude

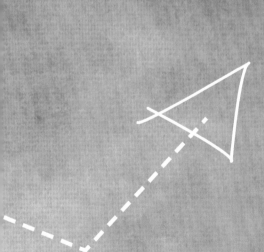

CHAPTER 9

Last but not least—
Contentment vs. gratitude

*O*ften, contentment and gratitude are viewed incorrectly. Both values are important in soccer and personal development.

1. Discontent as a driving force

"Good is bad when it could be better." – Kurt Maus—successful soccer coach for 50 years, currently for the team TSC Euskirchen

Discontent is a driving force to continuously improve and make progress, which is why a soccer player should never be satisfied.

2. Gratitude and humility

Contentment is often confused with gratitude and humility, and both of these values, in particular, are often not sufficiently developed in our longitudes and latitudes:

"I once cried because I had no shoes to play football with my friends, but one day I saw a man who had no feet, and I realized how rich I am."

Zinedine Zidane—world champion and two-time World Player of the Year

And, in keeping with legendary coach Giovanni Trappatoni (Champions League winner with Juventus Torino), who also uses tactical periodization in his training:

"I HAVE FINISHED."

PHOTO CREDITS

Cover design:	Andreas Reuel
Cover photos:	©imago-sportfotodienst
Jacket design:	Andreas Reuel
Layout:	Claudia Sakyi
Typesetting:	Andreas Reuel
Photos inside:	©Thinkstock/ChoochartSansong; chapter header; photo at top

©Thinkstock/iStock; chapter header; photo at bottom

©picture-alliance/dpa; pg. 11, 13, 14, 15, 29, 30, 31, 33, 36, 46, 49, 52, 58, 60, 62, 63, 66, 68, 78, 79, 82, 106, 116, 134, 140, 158, 159, 161, 164, 249

©picture-alliance/ZB; pg. 108

©imago-sportfotodienst;
pg. 10 (14868071h), 16 (09410323h),
22 (22094358h), 26 (09735463h), 30 (17661472h),
62 (19202561h), 66 (07729691h), 70 (07736446h),
72 (18044560h), 74 (13406707h), 101 (03730157h),
108 (13695711h), 122 (19138252h), 124 (16705892h),
127 (18013072h), 129 (18293601h), 133 (03502527h),
140 (19283295h), 141 (05921772h), 149 (14530854h),
166 (01318770h), 166 (18913942h), 170 (19355364h),

Pg. 91 & 96: ©Horst Wein

Graphics: easy Sports-Graphics

www.easy-sports-software.com

Editing: Elizabeth Evans

TRAIN LIKE THE WORLD CHAMPIONS

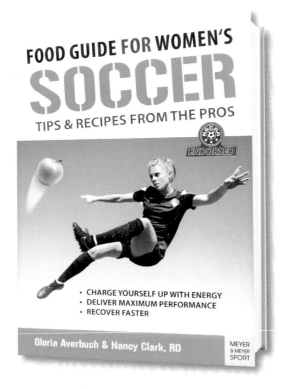

256 p., in color, 40 photos, 41 illus.,

paperback, 6 1/2" x 9 1/4"

ISBN 978-1-78255-051-8

$ 18.95 US/$ 32.95 AUS/£ 14.95 UK/€ 18.95

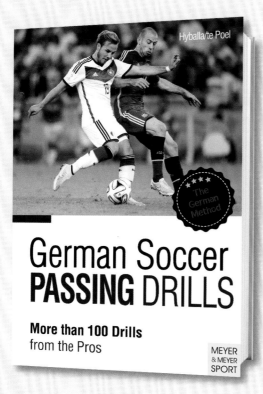

336 p., in color, 17 photos, 159 illus.,

paperback, 6 1/2" x 9 1/4"

ISBN 978-1-78255-048-8

$ 17.95 US/$ 29.95 AUS/£ 12.95 UK/€ 17.95

MEYER & MEYER
Sports GmbH
Von-Coels-Str. 390
52080 Aachen
Germany

Phone	02 41 - 9 58 10 - 13
Fax	02 41 - 9 58 10 - 10
E-Mail	sales@m-m-sports.com
Website	www.m-m-sports.com

All books available as E-books.

MEYER
& MEYER
SPORT